1-5-76

Studies In Ministry
And Parish Life

CONFLICT In A
Voluntary Association

A Case Study of a Classic
Suburban Church Fight

Edited By

Perry D. LeFevre

EXPLORATION PRESS

1975

Exploration Press
of
The Chicago Theological Seminary
5757 University Avenue
Chicago, Illinois 60637

ISBN: 0-913552-03-8

Library of Congress Catalog Card Number: 75-12388

1905445

Contents

Preface

The decade of the '60's was a time of controversy and conflict in American life. Polarization around social issues characterized both the nation and its institutions. The churches shared in what became the national ethos. At the same time the ferment in religious institutions went beyond the conflict over social issues. It was a time of new theological proposals, of widespread discussions of church renewal, and of the development of new patterns of church life aimed both at relevance to the new cultural and social situation and at revitalizing the internal life of Christian communities.

The original case study of the Elmhurst Church conflict, published in 1966, was designed to raise many of the issues confronting laity, clergy, and churches to the level of critical reflection. In putting together the original case history I was interested in producing as fair and dispassionate an account as possible. I hoped that congregations and clergy might see what happened at Elmhurst as a kind of paradigm and that the case study might be helpful as they dealt with similar issues in their own institutional life. My question was: What can we learn from what happened at Elmhurst?

It soon became apparent that the Elmhurst case study met a genuine need. The issue of the **Register** in which it appeared was so widely used that a second printing was necessary. Local congregations, state conferences, and ministers' groups ordered multiple copies. Individual clergy and lay persons ordered copies for friends. Seminary professors used the case as a text for class discussions. Indeed, one business school professor used copies of this issue of the **Register** in a course on conflict management.

By 1974 with the supply of copies of the Elmhurst case long since exhausted and requests and orders still coming in, the possibility occurred to me of re-issuing the case as a small book, with a supplement bringing the study up to date. What had happened in the nearly ten years since the original controversy? What did some of the leading participants now think about the conflict and the ensuing church split? How do they see the issue of church renewal a decade later?

I therefore asked the Rev. Don Stoner, formerly on the staff of First Church and a member of the Church of the Covenant to bring together a group of those best able to address such questions. The occasion was the Third Annual Professional Papers Conference at the Chicago Theological Seminary in April, 1974. The papers which they presented for group discussion are contained in Part III of this book.

In preparing the enlarged case study it seemed appropriate to include several additional reflections on the Elmhurst situation which had been published outside the original **Register** issue. The first of these by Ron Goetz appeared in **Renewal Magazine** at the time of the controversy. It was written in the heat of the struggle, as was the Church Council's response which followed in the next issue of **Renewal**. Dr. Goetz's new contribution to this book includes a retrospective comment on his earlier article. A third paper dealing with Elmhurst was written by Professor Charles Dailey and published in the **Register** issue of May, 1969 on conflict management. Professor Dailey's analysis is referred to by William Dudley in his new contribution to this book.

I have added an Appendix to the materials dealing with Elmhurst, drawn from the **Register** of December, 1969. These are further case studies of the church and ministry in conflict situations, and they include role-playing and psychodrama instructions as well as discussion questions.

The case materials in this small book are intended to open up discussion around four issues: a) the sociological and psychological understanding of the nature of conflict and conflict management, particularly in a voluntary organization; b) the nature and strategy of church renewal; c) the historical understanding of the ethos of the '60's; and d) the theological interpretation of the nature of the church and ministry and of church life in relation to the renewal movement.

I would like to thank all of the participants in the section of the 1974 Professional Papers Conference for their contributions. They have made possible what may be a unique document. There are, of course, an increasing number of case studies of problems in church life. Few, if any however, provide a ten-year follow-up of the original case material. I am especially grateful to Don Stoner for bringing the latter-day group together and for planning the structure of the discussion.

PERRY LeFEVRE, Editor

Part I
The Elmhurst Case Study

THE LOCAL CHURCH IN CRISIS

NOTICE OF SPECIAL MEETING

IN ACCORDANCE WITH ARTICLE 8, SECTION 2, OF THE CONSTITUTION OF THE FIRST CONGREGATIONAL CHURCH OF ELMHURST (UNITED CHURCH OF CHRIST), A BUSINESS MEETING IS HEREBY CALLED TO CONVENE IN THE MAIN SANCTUARY OF OUR CHURCH AT 12:15 P.M. NOVEMBER 7, 1965. THE PURPOSE OF THIS MEETING IS TO REQUEST THE RESIGNATIONS OF THE REVEREND WILLIAM H. DUDLEY AND THE REVEREND DONALD G. STONER, EFFECTIVE ON OR BEFORE FEBRUARY 7, 1966.

[The special meeting of the members of e church was duly held, and, after a mo- n concerning the form of the written llot to be used, a motion was proposed: o eliminate all debate and vote on the ue."]*

Mr. Dudley addressed the chair with e question: "Am I to be denied the right speak?"
Parliamentary ruling: According to rliamentary procedure, if the motion is ssed, the ministers, as well as anyone e, are indeed denied the right of debate. Ballots were distributed. Results of the lloting:

For the resignation of Mr. Dudley.. 245
Against the resignation of Mr. Dudley......................... 223

* Editorial continuity is bracketed. All other ma- al is quoted.

3. For the resignation of Mr. Stoner... 215
4. Against the resignation of Mr. Stoner 249

A request to speak was granted Mr. Stoner, who announced that his resignation would be forthcoming. . . . The Chairman of the Christian Social Action Board announced his resignation.

The Moderator declared that there might be more resignations forthcoming, and he wondered "if you realize what you have done. I don't know what I'm moderator of anymore. The congregation has created its image to the community and the ministerial profession. I hope you can live with it." His brief speech was greeted by a long round of applause.

ORIGINS OF CONFLICT

[The origins of tension and conflict in a local congregation are difficult to trace to

5

their roots. Much has to happen to individuals and to constituent groups before controversy moves to the point of a church meeting called to vote for or against the resignations of the church's professional leaders. Congregations, ministers, and prospective ministers need to try to understand the factors which create conflict and the processes by which such conflict is either moved to resolution and reconciliation or to rupture. It is the purpose of this study to trace as objectively as possible, through the documents themselves, what happened in the Elmhurst church, what efforts were made to handle tensions as they increased, and what the outcome was. We shall not editorialize; but, when the story is told without prejudice, we shall ask for a retrospective comment from representative participants and for an interpretative comment from one who is long-experienced in the life of our churches. It is hoped that this case study will help laymen and ministers alike to find ways of handling tension within our churches constructively—that they might more fully embody the spirit of the Christ.

IN MISSIONS

One of the earliest references in the official documents to a matter that appears to symbolize some of the issues that later came to divide the Elmhurst church is related to the work of the Stewardship and Missions Committee. The minutes of this committee for January, 1964, report a discussion of the possibility of separating the operating and benevolence pledges in the approach to the congregation for financial support. This discussion seems to indicate an intensification of interest and concern among a group in the church for a greater commitment to stewardship and missions. In April, 1964, the Stewardship and Missions Committee did bring this proposal to the Church Council, indicat-

ing that they hoped that a goal of 50 p cent "for ourselves" and 50 per cent " others" could be achieved. In order have this plan adopted, the Committee June requested a meeting with the Tru tees. The Board of Trustees in July vot the Committee's request down, holdi that such a plan "would probably result a reduction of Mission Pledges and t best interest of the church membersh would not be served." They felt that su a move would "have the effect of taki the handling of the mission money aw from the Board of Trustees which wou require an amendment to the Constit tion." They then went on to review t financial situation in these words:]

In 1960 we had 623 (six hundred twe ty-three) members pledging contributio to the church; in 1962, 551 (five hundr fifty-one); in 1964, 486 (four hundr eighty-six). This 1964 figure is a decrea of 22% as compared to 1960, and 11.8 compared to 1962, while at the same tir the population of Elmhurst increas from 37,500 to 40,330 an increase slightly in excess of 9%. The avera church attendance in 1960 was 602, 1962 548 and 1963—500. This would re resent a decrease of almost 17% over 19 and a little less than 10% compared 1962.

[The Board concluded its response the request of the Stewardship and M sions Committee in these words to t Church Council:]

In closing the Board of Trustees has resolution to offer for your consideratio Let us resolve to unite our activities in effort to find a way to bring the membe back to church, stimulate their interest they will actively participate in the a fairs of the Church and create renew interest, resulting in increased annu pledges.

6

[It appears from this interchange that some members of the church were pressing for a clearer-cut opportunity for commitment to the work of the church in the world and that the Trustees were sensitive both to their own prerogatives in the handling of money and to the financial problems which they felt were faced by the church as the result of a declining number of pledges and declining church attendance. The Trustees' action was reported to the Church Council, and the minister was moved to read a memorandum to the Council holding that the discussion of the matter had been "healthy." He went on to say that it was the system of operation that was to be questioned:]

The notion of mission giving as a "flexible absorber" is not good churchmanship. It suggests that mission giving may properly be considered *after* other expenditures and obligations.

[He added:]

As a principle of churchmanship, mission should not be determined by the relative needs of the operating budget.

[He then went on to reveal something of his own attitudes toward the self-preoccupation of churches, saying:]

The notion that the Church has just so much income no matter what we do is *somewhat* erroneous. There are people who are dissatisfied with the Church because it is so self-preoccupied, so institutional minded. Some of these people give generously to other causes because they feel they will do more good. A vigorous, vital, serving church should be the primary channel of giving for a committed Christian. I feel sure we deprive the Church of potential income because we do not stand for what the Gospel really means for the world.

The potential giving for our Church is several times over what is presently given.

I do not believe it a case of "*either* operating or *mission*."

[At the July meeting of the Council, the Chairman of the Board of Trustees read the prepared statement relating to membership, pledges, attendance, and other matters covering the period 1960–64. His statement provoked considerable discussion, and the Council passed a resolution creating a committee to be made up of the heads of the various church boards to consider the difficulties and dissatisfactions which seemed to be developing in the church.

IN CHRISTIAN EDUCATION

Meanwhile, the Christian Education Committee had been meeting to consider the program and building needs of the church in its own area. Its report, which the Committee approved on July 30, called attention to an earlier report (1960) on needs, indicating that the situation was substantially unchanged. In evaluating the situation, it raised certain questions about the interest of the congregation in the support of improvements. These questions reflect a growing awareness of division within the body of the church. The report says:]

Perhaps, too, our membership of long-standing has become complacent and is satisfied to have things continue as they are or to even regress to the "good old days." Certainly our facilities do not attract families. Compared to other church facilities in the community our facilities are near the bottom in terms of attractiveness, safeness, and over-all suitability for Christian Education purposes. It is known that some families have refrained from bringing their children here because of the facilities. The educational need, in terms of both committed leadership and desirable facilities, has not been met by the Church in terms of the present situation.

And further, we believe that we must catch up to the present in order to be prepared to meet the challenge of an expanding community in the future.

It is time for us to take a critical look at ourselves to ascertain the "active" membership of the Church and of those families who are actually committed to its program and to set our sights on its potential for the future. We have recently moved through a period of adjustment in our Church's life with a change in professional leadership, a new curriculum and confirmation program, new emphasis on the importance of adult education, and a new sense of mission which has made for changes in our program. The future holds the promise of new and deeper growth for us as a Christian Community.

A LAYMAN WRITES

[In the same month, one of the church members reflected on the "problems in our church" in the following document:]

The assignment is to try to identify problems in our church so we can more easily look for solutions. First, I will recite —at random—various "problems" I have heard from others—problems I do not entirely understand. My comments follow each problem.

Problem: Our church is now not "religiously conservative."

Comment: I take this to mean that some people don't like a change from past ways of church life. Do we want change or not?

Problem: Our church school attendance is declining. Some children do not like to attend; we haven't enough teachers.

Comment: Is attendance in fact declining? If there are not enough teachers, what's wrong with our congregation? I would guess that most objectors here are not teachers and really object to the demand to participate. They want a Sunday morning baby-sitting service.

Problem: Church attendance is declining.

Comment: Is it in fact declining? Even if it is, is the quality of our worship service better or not? And is the quality and quantity of total church participation improved or not? Without any way of "proving" this, I believe the overall vitality of our church is improving.

Problem: The race issue is too prominent; we are sending agitators to Mississippi against the wishes of and without approval by the church or church council.

Comment: I don't believe it can be too prominent—the race issue is clearly one of the most important moral problems of our age. To be vital the church must be deeply involved. Our Mississippi project was discussed and approved by the Council, after our commitment only because of timing.

Problem: The social clubs are being subverted, by lack of ministerial leadership.

Comment: I believe our ministers are merely not emphasizing the clubs, directing major attention to what they regard as more vital areas. This seems the essence of their ministry.

Problem: Demands are so great that the "less-committed" persons are alienated. Our ministers are pushing too fast for change. We must slow down and so draw in these persons, not push them out.

Comment: Certainly every member has had numerous opportunities to participate. I don't think our church would be hurt if "low commitment" people found a church more suited to their taste.

Problem: Cutting inactive members off the rolls is unfair—it is some of us sitting in judgment of others.

Comment: This is merely facing facts. No one is being pushed out; rather they are pointedly being asked to participate.

Problem: Separate mission budget pledges will eliminate the flexibility needed by the trustees to pay bills.

Comment: This may be, but why leave the cushion entirely in one budget? I believe we can work out a satisfactory compromise here, so the cushion is in both our operating and mission budgets.

Problem: The ministers are interfering unwarrantedly in choir affairs.

Comment: I don't think this is so. But certainly the music should be coordinated with the rest of the worship service.

Problem: Ministers are not making house calls.

Comment: I don't know the facts or the answer here.

Problem: A modern church should have a parking lot.

Comment: Sure. But what comes first? Shouldn't we be giving more than 10% of our total budget to others before we build a parking lot?

Problem: Our community hall is unsightly, unsafe, and inefficient.

Comment: Same as for parking lot.

What I think is going on in our church is that we are being asked to change from a suburban Sunday morning social club. We are forever being challenged with "What is the meaning of life?" "When we have life made materially, what do we do now?" Change and such questions are painful. We, I among them, are still stuck with the lesser goals of status and social class, material wealth, pleasures and political prejudice. This is a complex and interdependent world and there will always be differences. Our basic problem is to learn to put God first and so tolerate our lesser differences.

I want to be challenged with ultimate meaning. I want to find a way to organize my life on a more meaningful basis. I want to learn. So, I believe we should continue in our present direction, recognizing that this is *our* church and its problems are *ours* to find and solve. Questions and ferment in the open are healthy. Let's keep it this way. If some in the church do not like our present direction, let us continue to provide opportunities for them to join us, but not be shaken if they drift away.

[By this point, the issue of the leadership and direction of the church had been clearly raised. Some statistics on the pledging for 1964 and 1965 were offered, but no detailed analysis had yet been made. The pastor sought to meet this issue with a frank appraisal of the condition of the church and the church's relation to community changes. In a long memorandum read at the following Church Council meeting, he said:]

THE PASTOR SPEAKS

MEMO FOR COUNCIL COMMITTEE TO ACT ON RESOLUTION

1. Discussion and understanding concerning "the statistics of decline" is long overdue.
2. Comments on the statistics:
   a) The "Welcome Wagon" lists of newcomers are over 50% Roman Catholic. The next largest group is Lutheran. One cannot be sure that there will be even a single "Congregational" listing and only one or at most several "United Church of Christ" listings. The community is growing, but the increase is not composed of the people who would ordinarily "seek out" The First Congregational Church.
   b) During the time of community expansion Roman Catholic parishes have expanded. Also a United Church of Christ (Bethel) and strong Methodist and Presbyterian Churches have been established. My understanding is that some of the leadership of these churches came out of The First Congregational Church. There is no question but what these congre-

gations are composed of the kind of people who normally would be in First Congregational Church. The day when this was the only "liberal," "free," "community oriented" Church is past.

c) We live in a mobile society. Most of the attrition represented by a diminished number of pledges is due to moving or death. These people are not coming back. These people should not be confused with those who have been disaffected with the church and have not supported it for some time. Some discrimination needs to be exercised in the evaluation of "gripes."

d) The statistics quoted are for the years 1960, '61, '62, and '63. It should be noted that '60 and '61 were years during which a major break occurred in the life of the Church and two staff members were dismissed. This kind of shock is not conductive toward an upward trend either at the time it occurs or for some time after. There are people still using this as an excuse for non-support.

3. First Congregational Church does not have an outstanding sense of unity, community, mission, purpose, vital orientation to the Gospel, churchmanship, call it what you will. This is not the kind of thing that is nurtured by an assortment of "socially oriented Church clubs" or a "segmented" Church. Clubs are divisive—people tend to remain in their little little circle. Clubs do not create purpose—there is little common cause between clubs. Clubs do not generally attract outsiders in a community that is fairly well "clubbed."

This condition has prevailed for a long season and has tended to create a selective process through which persons of this disposition gravitate into positions of leadership and for that matter it tends to draw that kind of person into regular membership. This condition as part of the selective process resulted in the fact that many persons who lacked sufficiently strong ties were attracted to other churches in the community. This may be a reason why First Congregational Church is somewhat of an "older" congregation.

4. The physical facilities of the First Congregational Church are a handicap. Families with pre-school children need only compare the environment of "Community Hall" or the basement nursery, or even the combined crib and toddlers' room in the new building with the facilities of the Methodist or Presbyterian Churches, Bethel United Church of Christ, or St. Peter's.

In addition, each one of these churches plus the Episcopal and Roman Catholic Churches have well located and outstanding parking facilities. Arguments that "people should learn to walk" do not make sense in an automobile culture. Verne Pederson, mortician, said appropriately: He would be *dead* if he didn't have a parking lot. So does any businessman who intends to stay in business. So does virtually every "going" church in this community.

5. Parking lots and buildings don't make a church any more than a house makes a family. But the family requires adequate facilities. A family needs relationships in which members of the family realize understanding, affection and security. Something like this must happen in a church.

6. Our present strategy is:

a) To unify the over-all Church program through the Council and create a sense of common purpose. This means that vital, functioning boards are necessary if the Council meeting is to be more than reading reports.

b) To plan Church-wide events, i.e., Advent, Christmas, Lent, Easter, Christian Enlistment, Planning Conference, Special guests on Sunday, Special Giving, program and projects.

c) To develop a sense of mission—participation in God's work in the world—through "missions," Christian Social Action, etc.

d) To develop a community of devotion and learning through:

    (1) The development of responsible ministering boards of the Church. (This spells "laity," "ministry," "mission," etc.)

    (2) Sunday worship that is alive and meaningful.

    (3) Small (Devotional–Study–Self-Discovery) Groups.

    (4) Bible study.

    (5) Church School Teacher-Parent Training.

    (6) Pastoral counseling—pre-marital counseling, preparation of parents for infant baptism, etc.

This strategy is primarily directed to the cultivation and nurture of a "core group." There is no wisdom in a Board of Deacons, or Christian Education or Stewardship and Missions Board talking about developing the periphery until the board members themselves are prepared to provide leadership. To do otherwise is an excuse and assures failure.

. When a Church begins to "move," some people are disturbed. It is not those at the core of the church so much as those on the periphery who have maintained little, if any, active affiliation with the church in the past and who now use this as an excuse for inaction in the present.

8. The attrition of members we are now experiencing will continue until we develop a vital center—until some real changes have occurred—until the Church means enough in people's lives so that they feel compelled to share their experience with friends and neighbors.

The attrition of finances will be stemmed as we become more deeply involved and committed to the "mission" of the Church locally, and in the wider community.

No friendly resolution which does not take the above into account, and which thereby circumvents the real problem, can possibly solve the problem.

9. I am convinced that a strategy of avoiding the controversy of "being a Church," seeking to satisfy and mollify anyone who happens to have an objection and ordering the whole program to the lowest common denominator, will go nowhere, but down. The alternative is no guarantee of "success" but it is in the direction of "life."

10. Progress is painfully slow. Patterns do not change easily, or quickly, or without cost. The slowness is frustrating. I am able to struggle with it as long as there is some evidence of movement and progress. Where that is not possible I have no ministry. But to share with a people in a spiritual pilgrimage which finds its motivation and direction in response to the God of Jesus Christ is of all consuming importance. Wherever I am "called" or "sent" this is what I intend to do. It is the record of my ministry. This was made abundantly clear to the Pastoral

11

Committee and I want to reaffirm it now.

11. At the moment it is of supreme importance that the "core group" (the council) recognize the above implications and accept or reject them (with the possibility of modifications). A great deal of unnecessary misunderstanding and pain can thereby be averted.

PASTOR'S PRIVATE ANALYSIS

[At about the same time that the minister presented the preceding memorandum to the Church Council, he tried to set down privately his further analysis of "the problem" of First Church. This document was not published but was intended to be used to inform such persons as the Association Minister of the difficulties faced by staff and congregation.]

It is difficult to describe "the problem" of First Church. There is no specific issue. The "opposition" appears to be unorganized and inarticulate. But there is constant rumbling and apparently little capacity or desire on the part of "leadership" to move in any strong and affirmative way. "Don't rock the boat," is the watchword, and with that kind of support staff can extend itself just so far.

Meanwhile the attrition of membership through moving, retirement, and disenchantment (I believe in that order of importance) proceeds relentlessly. There is a small operating deficit for 1965 ($5,000–$8,000) which, even though it were to be covered for the current year, will undoubtedly appear in more serious proportions next year. The existence of the deficit has provided the occasion for a good deal of growsing, but little evidence of willingness to face the facts.

The three of us comprising the staff are of one mind. We see the situation deteriorating until such time as there is a concerted and determined effort to meet the problem constructively and cre tively. While we appear to have "reache quite a few individuals, there is relative little jelling into any kind of unity whi would resemble the "organism" of t church. The people "reached" do not re resent the "power structure" as it is rep sented by the Board of Trustees or t Women's Fellowship.

The enclosed statement was present at a recent Council meeting. It seemed receive general assent and some co mendation. It was incorporated in t minutes of the Council. Some of it is "u derstatement" as it was not intended be critical, controversial, or to open wounds, but simply to point up several the problem areas.

A succinct way of framing the proble is to quote the items listed in "The Lent Program for Adults" and "The School f Christian Living" (former programs this church) which appear as follows:

LENTEN PROGRAM

Old Testament Characters	Exploring Our Chr tian Concerns
Bowling	Agenda Group
Ceramics	Bait and Fly Cast
Puppets	Dramatics
Desire To Join the Church	Square Dance Gro

SCHOOL FOR CHRISTIAN LIVING

Church History	Mixed Bowling
Volley Ball	Bridge Instruction
Folk Dance Instruction	"Nite of Games": Ping-Pong, Shuf
Ceramics	board, Darts,
Furniture Refinishing	Chess, Backgam-
Fisherman's Hobby Group	mon, Checkers
	Leather Craft
Courageous Living	Square Dancing
Family Church Dinners	Interior Decorating
	Return to Religion

People who participated "faithfully" these programs somehow feel that th are being deprived of "personal religio

12

xperience," not because the staff has op-
osed doing any or all of these things (if
nyone has the desire and drive to organ-
e and pursue them), but because staff
as provided no leadership in these direc-
ons.

This part of staff time has been ab-
orbed in teacher recruitment and train-
ng, and developing program through the
Board of Christian Education; the devel-
pment of "small groups," Bible class,
dvent and Lenten programs; developing
he Diaconate so as to assume responsibil-
y for worship and the development of
piritual life; and working with the boards
f Social Action, Stewardship and Mis-
ons, and Evangelism so as to equip board
embers for a ministry to and through
he entire congregation.

A COUNCIL MEMBER SPEAKS

[An alternative analysis of the tensions
nd dissatisfactions within the church
hat nevertheless reflects the same sense of
growing division of the church's body
nto those "actively committed" to the
ntensified program of the ministerial
eadership and those felt by some to re-
ain on the "periphery" was presented at
Church Council meeting by one of its
embers. The text reads:]

For some time now, I have been review-
ng in my own mind the many concerns
egarding our church. For some reason or
ther, many of our members have come to
e expressing similar concerns. I feel that
he concerned are not a minority group.

I have tried to evaluate all these con-
ersations, but in the final analysis, al-
hough I agree with many of the com-
ents, the remarks I am about to make
re strictly personal, but I am compelled
o make them. I might add that Lee con-
urs with this paper.

I have not looked forward to this mo-
ent, nor do I expect this Council or the
Ministers to agree with all that I say.
However, this is the place for a member of
this church to express his thoughts. My
remarks will be those of a constructive
criticism, complete with comments and
proposals.

As a member of this church Council, I
feel it my responsibility to speak out to
this group concerning the vital issues with
which our church is faced today. We are
the so-called "core" of the church, the
members of the various boards which com-
prise the Council, the real working-wor-
shipping-giving members of the church. It
has been said that we 90-some people and
a few others of the church membership,
along with the three-member ministerial
staff, represent approximately 75% of the
financial aid and the real "life of the
church."

As a member from the Board of Christian Education, it has been a part of my
personal responsibility to share with you
in the actions and the inactions of this
council in the past few years. It is my understanding that our responsibility is to
share together in the works of the various
boards represented here, and to act as one
body to provide the leadership, to set the
policies for the whole working theme of a
United Church, and to communicate these
efforts to all the members of this church.
It is our responsibility to speak out at
these meetings, both pro and con on any
issue, to give constructive criticism to the
ministerial staff and on the actions of the
various boards. It is here that the ministers can speak out to the council in like
manner. This is the place where the council, the ministers, and interested church
members can meet each month and freely
discuss mutual problems, share in the joys
of progress, and in every way gain from
the free common bonds that we all should
so earnestly desire and aspire to.

It is also our responsibility to be astute
enough to bring into these meetings the

feelings and thoughts expressed to us by other members of this church.

This, then, is the place where we establish the common meeting ground, the level of mutual understanding upon which we start to build.

I have had the growing feeling that we have not fulfilled these responsibilities . . . a feeling that we have merely established a low-level, cloistered situation—*an island*. And the people on the mainland are referred to as the "periphery." Are we really here to sit in judgment and to agree that those in the periphery are really not worth bothering about??? Are we to accept as fact, if it is a fact, that these people who represent about 60% of our parish and who contribute approximately 25% of our budget are only the dissenters and the disgruntled???? And if this is the case, then does this not imply that here in itself we have a ministry? Should we not think in terms of a total congregation . . . or beyond that . . . to suggest that our ministry is to the entire population of Elmhurst and surrounding areas????

The problems and lives of the people of this community are varied to as great an extent as the people we are reaching through our United Church's "unstructured ministries." In such places as Oak Brook Center, the Strip in Las Vegas, Squaw Valley, industrial sites, and a church in the laundry room of a Pittsburgh high-rise apartment building, this contemporary approach is much the same as Christ's own ministry . . . talking to the people, the prostitute, the high priest, the tax collector. And just as Jesus approached every level of man, these special ministers are reaching the factory worker, the housewife, the prostitute, the business man, the homosexual, the skid row alcoholic or suburban alcoholic, and just plain people with ordinary and complex problems within their own environment. But what of the parish minister? Does he seek

out *his* people in their environment Don't we have the same varieties of peopl and problems?

The twentieth-century ministry o Christianity must be contemporary i every respect, with room for tomorrow problems. I believe that Christ's ministr on earth was a philosophy of life in man relationship with God *when* He taught i as well as being so true and relevant tha each succeeding generation of man fine it as a contemporary way of life, with a understanding of our God, Christ, Ma and the Church.

We are all familiar with those for words. But if we merely mouth thes words as a slogan, and then preach an practice a *limited* Christianity, we ar only practicing a second-century Christia ministry . . . forty years behind the time in a twentieth-century world.

I believe that this council must shou der part of the blame for the presen status of our church, simply because w have not expressed our thoughts and opir ions on ideas and methods right here i public forum. Mr. Dudley has presented package deal or format for practicin Christianity which has not been properl challenged, but which many of us feel ha not worked.

Evidence of this declining situation ha been mounting. We are at a point wher this council and all interested member whether so-called core or peripher should join together in serious discussio in these meetings and offer our constru tive criticism of our total program.

Just as we want and expect strong lea ership and guidance from our ministe . . . I feel sure *they* must want and expec to learn of our needs, our ideas, and ou dissatisfactions.

I believe that only through this mediu of open discussion can we as a congreg: tion express ideas, establish commo goals, broaden and deepen our relatior

14

ip with each other . . . and in a sense,
rite a new chapter to the New Testa-
ent here in Elmhurst.

In order for this to become possible, it
ill be necessary for our ministers to learn
 be more flexible in their thinking—and
r this council to be equally as flexible . . .
ıt above all, our thinking must be mu-
al and our actions consistent with our
cisions.

I should like to present to this council
e following proposals for our considera-
n, discussion, and action tonight:

1. That the First Congregational
hurch of Elmhurst be concerned with all
ople within the community of man.
hat we reject the notion that this church
nsists of a Christian Core and a Periph-
y. That we will reach out to all people,
ember or nonmember, regardless of their
ntributions, attendance, activity, or
y combination thereof, with Christian
derstanding and compassion. That we
ll respect the temple of God within each
an, and accept the intelligence and sin-
rity of their personal decisions.

2. That this church expand its pro-
am to the broadest scope, providing a
llowship within reach of all people, of all
es, and of all circumstances. That we
ree to abandon ideas which prove to be
rong, and that we have the vision to cre-
e new ideas. That we can deal with the
ienated as well as the satisfied, in order
 make our fellowship grow instead of
rink.

3. That our ministers reach out in ev-
y way possible to learn to know the
ople of this church . . . that they espe-
ally seek out the people, whether at
me, work, play, or in the church, not
ly to know them, but to understand
em in mutual respect and love.

4. That we form a Sunday evening dis-
ussion group, preferably a large group, to
t in open discussion on the topic and con-
nt of the morning sermon. That through

this, each person will have the opportunity to answer in agreement or rebuttal,
to gain greater depth of the subject, and
to share his own analogies with those
drawn by the minister in the text. These
can be meetings of mutual benefit . . . for
the Sermon Critics on the one hand—and
on the other hand, a help to the minister
in preparing future sermons.

These proposals are, of course, just a
few of my own suggestions. I hope that
this paper will help to draw out other suggestions, and to stimulate and encourage
serious discussion. My sincere desire is
that we as a church can finally start to
work together again. I believe in our people, and I also believe that we have ministers who are well qualified and capable. I
find it difficult to believe that we cannot
join together . . . not just in the "life of
the church" but to make this church LIVE.

FINANCIAL PROBLEMS

[Financial matters continued to reflect
deepening conflict in the church. The
Chairman of the Board of Trustees prepared a report in which he said:]

It is my duty as chairman of the Board
of Trustees to inform you of the current
financial position of your church.

As indicated in our letter of January
19th, this congregation is faced with a
critical situation. Our recent financial drive
did not develop the money currently required to present a balanced budget for
1965. Our present response to this crisis
will determine our course for several years
to come.

[After reviewing the budget, he declared that expected income fell short of
the budget by $7,885. He raised the ques-
tion of possible alternatives, and, in dealing with one of them, he commented:]

The Christian Investment committee
has informed the Board of Trustees that

15

... many members of the church have reduced or withheld pledges as a means of indicating dissatisfaction with the *staff leadership*. The Christian Enlistment Committee recognizes that there will inevitably be some degree of dissatisfaction with staff leadership in any church, more at some times than at others, and more in some churches than in others. The committee, however, feels that withholding financial support from both the local institution and the wider mission of the church is a most inappropriate way of registering dissatisfaction. A pledge should be part of an individual's considered response to God. To utilize it as an instrument of dissension is to distort its meaning. Furthermore, it should be pointed out that the church constitution makes adequate provision for the proper registering of opposition to staff procedures and policies. Nevertheless, we at this point, must accept the reality of the present which is that a substantial number of pledges have been decreased and withheld *primarily as a means of registering dissatisfaction with the present course of our church life*.

If the real issue dividing the church, or more accurately, strangling the church at the present time is concerned with staff procedure and policy then this issue should be debated openly on its merits rather than being *treated as a budgetary item*. It is perfectly clear that this issue must be met if we are to avoid sabotaging our own effort and in the process rendering our local institution a totally ineffective operation with no vitality to recover and perform its important function for its members and our community.

[Meanwhile, the special committee of board chairmen, established the preceding July to look into the problems facing the church and to establish communication, had apparently been relatively inactive. Because of the discussions provoked by the report of the Chairman of the Board of Trustees, the special committee was instructed to continue its attempt to "develop fuller communication with our members."]

THE PASTOR'S ANALYSIS

The minister went still further in the February, 1965, meeting of the Council with a public statement that attempted both to get at the facts related to finances and attendance—the so-called statistics of decline—and to spell out ways of dealing with this situation. In the latter section he clearly discloses something of his own conception of the nature and role of the local church and the direction of his leadership, which was under attack.]

The year-by-year record of the number of pledges and the number of worshipers from 1958 to the present is as follows:

	Number of Pledges	Number of Worshipers
1958	674	633
1959	640	602
1960	626	602
1961	530	507
1962	552	548
1963	513	500
1964	493	447

The horizontal line marks the beginning of the present pastorate. It will be noted that the yearly downward step was reversed one year, but continued steadily in 1963 and 1964, and from present indications will be the pattern for 1965. The long-term trend would suggest that it is not simply a matter of leadership. The 1963 pledges were made within nine months of the beginning of the present pastorate when it was anticipated that "new leadership" would release sources of income previously withheld. This was before it was conceivable that there could have been any "massive resistance or protest against the present administration."

The amount of dollars pledged for these years is also instructive:

1958	$75,588.00
1959	82,534.00
1960	90,264.00
1961	80,196.00
1962	82,942.00
1963	94,307.00
1964	94,624.00

The obvious conclusion is that fewer people have given more dollars. The dollars given are not necessarily directly related to the number of pledges. The answer to our problem is not simply "numbers."

Let us consider some of the explanations of the above figures.

1. Since the war there are a number of new and vigorous churches in this community. First Congregational Church is no longer "the only place to go" if you represent the liberal Protestant tradition. In some instances our own members living in "outlying districts" find new churches building on their own street which are far more convenient to attend or "send the children."

2. Roman Catholic activity has vastly increased. Well over half the newcomers to this community are presently listed as Roman Catholic. This is relatively new.

3. The physical facilities—especially for pre-school children (involving younger families)—parking lot, and general condition and appearance of the building do not present a strong appeal as compared to the new or renovated facilities of other churches. Pre-school parents who have any understanding of pre-school Christian education are not favorably impressed with Community Hall or the basement room next to the furnace, or with the crib room, as adequate or attractive educational facilities.

In this light it is apparent that the "new addition" was not built for Christian education in the broad sense. It was built for youth. The design of it and especially the choice of facilities (i.e., chapel) suggest a separation from the life of the total church. This was also expressed in staff and organization. The building itself and its furnishings do not express real commitment to the best concepts of Christian education.

4. The National Council of Churches Yearbook reveals that 1958 was the peak post-war year for church attendance. Beginning with 1958 the following percentages of church members attended church each year: "49, 47, 47, 46, 46, 45—a clear downward trend." Says the *Christian Century:* "We can speculate: boredom may be a factor; mere affiliation may satisfy many since affiliation is a part of the American Way of Life; some people may be reacting to the new social messages of the pulpit; distractions of the new leisure may woo some from worship."

5. National statistics for 1964 reveal that couples ages 25–54 are 19% of total population. In 1975 they will again be 50%. This reflects the decline in the birth rate during the depression years.

It means, however, that in communities like Elmhurst where a generally high economic level automatically restricts the number of young families that their number will be fewer still in the light of these national statistics. For the present and immediate future, established churches in established communities will inevitably have a lower percentage of "young families."

6. We should note that an increasing number of families are involved with "second homes" which occupy attention throughout the year. Also, there is more leisure for travel and sports. Many more families take winter vacations than formerly. Some of the men of the church travel widely for business reasons and are often absent over weekends. This cannot be tabulated, but it has a place in the in-

terpretation of statistics. Add to this the high mobility of American families which, for the church, automatically spells out the necessity of a high evangelistic index.

7. The First Congregational Church reflects an aging process. Generally speaking, the congregation is "older." Many people are at, or near, retirement. Families have grown up. This affects number of pledges, worship attendance, and church school figures. In addition, the organizations of the church have aged. Patterns have become set. In a younger church a "Merry-Mixers" organization studies Tillich or the mission theme of the denomination. In another generation, without strong leadership, they will settle into a socially oriented "in-group." This is characteristic of the pattern of church life. For the most part the process has been going on longer in First Church than in some of the newer churches.

8. A "Community House Philosophy" has characterized First Church from its inception. This filled a very definite need in a new and growing community. Today the community is organized to the hilt. The church cannot compete on this level. Besides, we are living in a new world with a new theological climate. Change in this direction is bound to create turbulence.

9. Some of the "community leaders" who have been members of First Church have supported the church on a "sponsorship basis." It reflects the notion that a church is a good institution to have in a community—it should be supported for the good it does. This attitude does not create "Christian community." It values the church in its institutional terms.

10. First Church has been a "minister-centered" church. The minister has "taken care of things." Lay responsibility for teaching, giving, witnessing, believing has not been emphasized. It has been a ministry with emphasis on institutional care-taking.

11. Many of the above factors seem [?] have contributed to a "segmented" church. In many instances youths hav[e] been drawn in without parents or wit[h] nominal parent support of the church du[r]ing the years of the youth's involvemen[t]. The youth program has been apart fro[m] the life of the church. Through the Wom[en's] Fellowship women have become pa[rt] of the church without their husbands. I[n] some instances individuals and coupl[es] have found their church affiliation pr[i]marily through club membership. Som[e] children are "sent" to the church schoo[l]. All in all, this tends to detract from Chri[s]tian community—one church family sha[r]ing in a common belief, understandin[g] and service.

These are some of the factors that u[n]derlie the statistics of decline, and it seem[s] reasonable that the trend will continu[e] until enough of the conditions are mod[i]fied. Realistic ways of dealing with cond[i]tions reflecting a downward trend [in] pledges and worshipers are as follows:

1. Worship and spiritual life must fin[d] new levels of meaning and relevance. [A] program of education and cultivatio[n] needs to be conducted by the Diacona[te] for all members of the parish. Worship i[t]self needs to be re-ordered and rendere[d] fresh and relevant. The rearrangement [of] the chancel is a case in point. The cultiva[tion] tion and nurture of "Small Groups" (Spi[r]itual Life, Self-Discovery, Dialogu[e] Groups, etc.) is another approach. Th[e] whole Church Family (Church Schoo[l] parents, teachers, youth, Women's Fe[llowship] lowship, Church Council, the Boards an[d] the pulpit) needs to grapple together wit[h] the basic questions of our life and fait[h]. ("The Christian Observance of Life['s] Great Events" is an attempt to expan[d] the dialogue of concern.)

2. Attendance and commitment wi[ll] follow when a dedicated core of Churc[h]

18

School teachers, youth leaders, Board of Christian Education members, and the pulpit are able to engage parents and all members of the church in the dynamics of Christian growth and understanding. This is a slow, painful process. Responsible, mature relationship between the church family and the youth and the Church School, or between the parents and the teachers is an element that, with certain exceptions, has been seriously lacking.

3. The church must bear a relevant witness. People need to feel they are part of something significant. We lose support for the church more because we stand for so little, than because we serve some cause that is relevant to life.

This means that Stewardship will have to interpret the use of our money and enlist real—not token—commitment to the mission of the church. It means that Social Action is going to have to move with strength and provide leadership. It means that lay people will have to grow in such understanding and commitment to the faith that they have no other alternative than to share it with their neighbors and draw them into the fellowship.

This will not happen by following the admonitions of those who are presently uncommitted, or who are thoroughly fixed and rooted in "the good old days" and want no growth or change. For this reason it becomes essential that "membership in the church" mean at least as much as "assent to the Church Covenant." This is the only basis of our life together. Persons who will not worship, who do not choose to grow intellectually in the understanding of the faith or make a responsible commitment for the support and mission of the church, reject the Covenant—they withdraw from the fellowship. (This does not mean all must agree in every thought, and assent to a set creed or dogma, but there is a need to express a willingness to share in worship, growth, and service together.) Those who do not honor the Covenant but are continued as members of the institution provide a constant source of negation and dissipate the energies of the fellowship.

A suggestion would be "not to throw them out," but to consider the possibility of two categories: "*Members*," and "*Those to be cultivated and loved*." No one puts anyone out on a holier-than-thou basis. But an army, or a family, or a church, has to have a fairly clear idea as to who will be part of the fellowship, who will cooperate, who will share, who will serve. And when it comes to choosing directions and making decisions, whose insights and concerns will be expressed.

Many people are lost to the church because of the weak, vacillating, empty quality of church life. Those who are of the household of faith have a great responsibility at this point. The responsibility is to those who are seeking, and then it turns to those who are not seeking.

When a church develops a strong community of dedicated people, this in itself tends to carry along a lot of partial, half-commitment that would otherwise go nowhere.

Without self-righteousness, without being judgmental, without being exclusive, legalistic, or assuming any negative or contemptuous attitude, a church family needs to order its spiritual life, and fashion some disciplines that make a clear difference as to whether one is a "member of the family," or one that should be "cultivated and loved."

This issue is one of the clearest tests of whether a church family will be led and enriched by the committed, or whether it will adhere to the pattern of the least common denominator—and, in the end, be nothing.

19

COMMITTEE'S REPORT

[A congregational meeting was held early in April, 1965, at which a report was given that ninety-two families had increased their pledges by $7,276, to meet the threatened deficit. At the same time it was voted to distribute the two analyses (the minister's "white paper," as it was called, read at the February Council meeting, and the earlier "November paper" read to the Council) to the whole church and to call a special congregational meeting one month later to consider "the problems of the church."

Later in the month a special committee of the chairmen of the various church boards, which had been appointed the previous July to study the "extent and causes for alleged member dissatisfaction," made its report to the Church Council. The pertinent excerpts from the report (later distributed to all church members) follow:]

EXHIBIT NO. 1—APRIL 6, 1965

Excerpts from the Report of the Committee of Board Chairmen

At the July 16, 1964, meeting of the Council, a motion was made and passed that a special committee composed of the chairmen of all boards of the church be formed to investigate and make appropriate recommendations concerning an alleged high degree of congregational dissatisfaction with the current program and stance of the church. The committee of board chairmen has met each month since July (1964) and has studied and discussed the problems of the church at great length.

In trying to determine the extent and causes for this alleged dissatisfaction, the committee has used several sources of information, including the following:

1. Yearly record of pledges including number of pledges and total amount pledged.
2. Record of attendance at Sunday worship services.

3. Number of families not making a pledge and the reasons given.

The first two of these three source have been analyzed and reported on adequately to the council. This committee i in substantial agreement that decline in number of pledges and number of Sunday worshipers is due to population trends, decrease in number of non-Catholics moving into Elmhurst, increase in number of other churches in Elmhurst, diminished appeal of physical facilities, nationwide pattern of decline in church attendance and other factors.

This committee also studied the comments written on Christian Enlistment cards of some families who did not pledge in 1965 for the first time. The number of first-time pledge discontinuations in 1965 is 51. The reasons given by these 51 families for not pledging can be grouped as follows:

Moving	10
Protest	8
Transferring to other churches	4
Retirement	4
Deceased	1
No reason given	24

If even half of the families who gave no reason for not pledging were included with the "protests," the total number might be as high as 20.

While 10 to 20 pledges withheld as protest do represent a small but noteworthy expression of opposition to current church program, it is of even greater significance that pledge-withholding was used as a means of registering protest. . . .

Therefore, having studied and discussed the extent and causes for dissatisfaction in the church, this committee concludes that:

1. Complaints have tended to be vague and have often been expressed irresponsibly as through pledge-withholding. Also, there seems to be no broad

20

area of agreement between dissenters that can be answered responsibly by this committee. Therefore, this committee recommends that the church continue to encourage *all* members to participate in the life of the church through worship, learning, and service; and to grow together in Christian understanding, commitment, and love.

Our church needs to better understand its purpose, its mission, its reason for being, in order to move with love and conviction as the Body of Christ in the world.

THE COMMITTEE
OF BOARD CHAIRMEN

[This report did not resolve the tensions, and a further attempt at solution followed. A special four-man subcommittee of the Board of Deacons was established "for the purpose of conducting a greater depth study among those members who wished to express their dissatisfaction and their reasons for same." Time precluded a similar study of the views of those who were satisfied with the church's program.

This committee's report was accepted by the Diaconate on May 20, 1965. Pertinent excerpts (later circulated to the congregation) are as follows:]

EXHIBIT NO. 2

Excerpts from the Report of Special Diaconate Committee

A total of 167 members of the congregation communicated directly with this committee in this period. 22 more have indirectly communicated with us. Many of these people are frequently seen in attendance at church including members of the Board of Trustees, Diaconate, Choir, Board of Christian Education and other official church organizations.

The grievances and suggestions fell into a few general categories with varying degrees of repetition and emphasis. Your committee has endeavored to objectively report them and list specific grievances by the area of responsibility where possible.

A. Board of Christian Education
   1. General dissatisfaction with the present confirmation program. Confirmation should be made at the junior high level.
   2. There is a general feeling that the youth church should be reinstated, and strengthened.
   3. Some members believe Mr. Stoner is not doing a good job, as is evidenced by lack of attendance and interest on the part of our youth.
   4. It was suggested that social activities should be encouraged to which to bring children and which will provide opportunity for spiritual development.
   5. There is some dissatisfaction with the use of modern art in the curriculum.

B. Board of Christian Social Action
   1. There is a general feeling that this Board does not represent the true attitude of the congregation on large issues.
   2. Minority views of the congregation should be given more consideration.
   3. A major effort of the Board should be to educate the congregation on social issues.
   4. Time should be spent on issues other than the race issue.
   5. The Church should define this Board's responsibilities.

C. Lack of Social Activities
   1. There is a general feeling that all social activities are discouraged by the staff. Particular concern was expressed for the Women's Fellowship, Men's Club and Leisure-ites.
   2. There is a strong feeling that social activities create and maintain a friendly atmosphere and should be encouraged rather than discouraged.
   3. There is a need for activities and entertainment such as church suppers which will embrace the entire family.

D. United Church of Christ Affiliation
   1. There is a feeling we have lost independ-

ence in our affiliation with the United Church of Christ.

2. Many members feel our program is dictated by the United Church of Christ.

3. Other churches affiliated with the United Church of Christ are reported to be presenting their program without antagonizing their membership.

E. Organizational Practices

1. There is a general feeling that we lack "two-way communication" between the boards, the congregation and the ministers.

2. There is dissatisfaction with the long delay in such matters as revision of the constitution, questions involving maintenance of facilities and on new additions, and parking needs of the church.

3. Mr. Vonfeld's functions were questioned.

4. There is a general feeling that the boards and committees are dominated by the ministerial staff.

F. Sermons

1. People do not understand the sermons.

2. New theology is hard to grasp. It destroys old concepts and leaves nothing in their place.

3. Sermons are too repetitive in theme—too much emphasis on race and poverty—criticism but no comfort.

4. Sermons are not inspirational—too sarcastic.

G. Attitude of Ministers

1. Lack of personal warmth and friendliness on the part of Mr. Dudley and Mr. Stoner is the most frequent complaint. Members feel Mr. Dudley should *want* to make pastoral calls to become better acquainted.

2. There is lack of concern for those who do not accept Mr. Dudley's ideas.

3. Ineptness in personal relations on the part of Mr. Dudley and Mr. Stoner is apparent.

4. There is severe criticism of the labeling of the congregation as "core or periphery," "committed or non-committed," etc.

5. There was evidently lack of concern when the church showed evidence of disunion.

6. There is an intolerance of diverge opinions.

7. There is a lack of personal support social activities, particularly of t Women's Fellowship.

EFFORTS TOWARD RECONCILIATIO

[A congregational meeting followed o May 23, where an attempt was made t review and respond to the major areas c complaint. The Church Council meetin four days later again returned to the prob lem, and a committee was asked to pre pare a statement to the congregation. Th statement, dated June 2, included th quoted excerpts from the two committe reports and statements by the Moderato the Chairman of the Diaconate, and th Minister. These statements were designe to enlist co-operation and promote unit and healing in the church. Particularl significant passages follow:]

To All Church Members:

The *future* of the First Congregationa Church of Elmhurst is in *jeopardy*. Ou church is confronted with a serious problem of a continuing and growing dissatisfaction on the part of a segment of ou membership. While our problem is no necessarily considered to be unique among Protestant churches today, there is, however, one specific difference. This difference stems from the fact that this happens to be *our* problem and *our* church. Therefore, it is only natural that we should feel a greater degree of personal concern over its impact on the daily lives of each of us as individuals.

We sincerely believe that this type of problem cannot be successfully resolved by either ignoring it or by merely wishing or hoping that somehow everything will work out all right. Neither do we believe that such a problem can be resolved by engaging in any precipitous action which is not properly related to views and desires f the total membership and the true purpose of the Church of Jesus Christ. . . .

In an effort to provide a constructive basis for our future joint efforts in this matter the enclosed brief statements set forth the views and the respective positions of the moderator, the chairman of the diaconate and the minister of our church.

We are hopeful that the above statements will constructively contribute to each member's understanding of the problem. However, as your Moderator, your Chairman of the Diaconate, and your Minister, it would be completely impossible for us, without the willing cooperation of you and every other member of the congregation, to attain our mutual goals.

We feel confident, however, that if each one of us will exercise more individual restraint, patience and tolerance of differing viewpoints and will work together, with God's help we *can* and *will* find the answers we are seeking to the problems resulting from our human inadequacies.

MODERATOR
CHAIRMAN OF DIACONATE

STATEMENT OF THE MODERATOR

As Moderator, I share your deep concern for the lack of unity in our church, and for ministering to all of its members. I acknowledge my shortcomings and the limits of my ability in dealing with these problems. I ask you to bear with me in working out the solutions. I have given my best efforts and pledge to continue them in carrying out the responsibilities of my office. The Constitution of the Church gives the Moderator very limited responsibilities. However, I accept the following additional responsibilities as part of my job:

. Be impartial.
. Hear the views of all members.

3. Correlate the work of all boards to fulfill the mission of the church.

I assure you that each of the matters listed in the report of the four-man committee (Exhibit No. 2) will be explored in detail by the responsible board to determine what changes in program can be made, consistent with desires of the majority of members and the mission of the church. One board has already started such a review. The others will start as soon as possible.

MODERATOR

STATEMENT OF THE MINISTER

Let me share with you my concern for the lack of understanding and unity in our church. *Concern* is too mild a word. *Agony* and *pain* come closer to it. I begin to feel something of the loneliness and heartache of our Lord when looking upon the people of Jerusalem; he said: "How often would I have gathered your children together as a hen gathers her brood under her wings, and you would not" (Matthew 23:37b).

Speaking to the "criticisms" of my "sermons" and "attitudes" which have been specifically catalogued, let me express my failure to communicate the love of God and my failure as a *person* to meet *persons* in our ministry together. Let me acknowledge my limited powers of articulation, my limited knowledge and abilities for "implementing" the Christian faith in ways that would be acceptable to all, or to be more realistic, in ways that would assure greater acceptance and participation. I am very mindful of my limitations at this point and confess the need of a great deal of acceptance, forbearance and help as I struggle to follow the *Way* of Christ and make it known.

There are many ways in which the Church can function. Any one of a hundred New Testament images of the church

23

provides clues and direction. I am eager to change and grow with the congregation, using any one or all of these images as a guide. Ideas and suggestions will be most welcome.

However we structure it, the experience of God's love and forgiveness, the understanding of His will and a willingness to be used by Him is primary and essential.

I grow in the realization that my real need and the need of every person is for God's acceptance and forgiveness. Only upon the foundation of this experience grasping our hearts, minds and whole beings can our fellowship with each other and our own self-acceptance become more than a sentimental gesture.

The major theme of my ministry with you has been mainly in the direction of serving as the instrument for "calling" and "equipping" persons for their ministry to the entire fellowship and through the fellowship to all the world.

That this has been slow, painful, tedious and in so many ways "unsuccessful" is painfully evident. It reveals my inadequacies for which I pray God's help and yours. It reveals the fact that God's Holy Spirit has been so dreadfully limited in our fellowship together.

The potentialities God has given us for acceptance, meaning and usefulness are tremendous, but the tragedy for us all is that we have left them unclaimed.

MINISTER

STATEMENT OF CHAIRMAN OF THE DIACONATE

The Diaconate of the First Congregational Church of Elmhurst is faced as of May 30, 1965, with a grave responsibility but a challenging opportunity. Our membership has been divided by lack of understanding as to methods and motives. This has expressed itself in withdrawal of support both in money and in participation worship and serving. When man becomes confused, disenchanted and finally resentful of conditions around him, he rebels and in a church the leadership of church is attacked, usually the minister.

As the Diaconate sees these prevailing conditions, we also see an opportunity try in the best way we know how to seek out means to structure these forces in the direction of creating what the "church" needs should be. In listening to and discussing the many statements and dissatisfactions that have come to my ear past months, nothing is more abundantly clear than this: the congregation generally wants similar goals, but we stumble over ways to get these goals, and over definitions and interpretations of words.

I believe the following lines taken from the book *New Life in the Church*, by Robert A. Raines, a Methodist minister Germantown, Pennsylvania, provide some insight into our problem and offer food for thought and careful consideration:

The first thing to reaffirm is that we must stick with the church. As someone has remarked: "The church is like Noah's Ark; if it weren't for the storm outside, you couldn't stand the smell inside." There is a storm outside, and the church, pervaded as it is with the smell of genial paganism, is still the ark of salvation, and there is no other.

The second thing to reaffirm is that by ourselves we cannot do anything about it. We men are powerless to start revivals. We cannot schedule or blueprint or conjure into being the reviving Spirit of God. The Holy Spirit, like the wind, comes when and where He wills. So with men, it is impossible.

The third thing to reaffirm is that with God all things are possible. And in fact, the most exciting truth of our generation is that God has already started something! This is the tremendous experience we are having in our different ways. The Holy Spirit is loose again in the world, lives are changing; the church

24

being reborn and renewed in place after place; a new Pentecost as of the days of the early church is at hand. So our privilege and obligation are not to start a revival; rather, to watch for the tide rolling in, to catch it, to seek to ride with it, and to make new channels for these rivers of grace. We are to be instruments for the Holy Spirit who is awakening us and breathing His power into our sleeping churches. Quite specifically, it is the job of Christian laymen and ministers to create the conditions for conversion within the life of the local church. It is God who converts lives; it is we who are called to create the conditions of conversion.

Chairman of the Diaconate

STUDENT CONCERN

[In the midst of the rising tempo of debate within the church, it is interesting to note that a group of Elmhurst College students felt moved to address a letter of concern to the Church Council. The letter signed by fifty-four students follows:]

Mr. Dudley:

This we feel is the least we could do in light of all you have done for us. Fifty-four students signed the original—a small sampling of those who would have signed had there been time for ample circulation of the letter.

Elmhurst College
Elmhurst, Illinois
May 30, 1965

Church Council
First Congregational Church
United Church of Christ
Elmhurst, Illinois

Gentlemen:

Many of us here have been disturbed by what we understand is happening at First Congregational concerning the pastors and Mr. Vonfeld and the church's relationship to the United Church of Christ.

We realize that in light of the opposition the pastors face, our influence is small; yet we wish to express our appreciation for their service to our college community, the larger community of Elmhurst, and the Church Universal. We, as students, have been fortunate to learn from and be challenged by the ministers of your church in their attempts to comfort the afflicted and afflict the comfortable. It is difficult to perform a relevant ministry, but your ministers have taken Christianity seriously and have caused all of us to do the same. Elmhurst College, the larger community of Elmhurst, and the Church of Jesus Christ need men of this calibre and sensitivity, and we would consider their leaving a great loss.

We urge that you support these men, taking a firm stand on the issues dividing the congregation. To remain silent is to condone the actions of the opposition.

Respectfully,

The Undersigned Students of
Elmhurst College

[Something of the minister's feelings about the local situation and his views of the larger question of the meaning of the church are revealed in his letter of response to an inquiry from a State Conference outside Illinois regarding his willingness to consider moving. He wrote:]

. . . My willingness to consider such a prospect which may involve a radical cut in income, staff, etc., is with the thought that such new ventures might well provide opportunities for the development of a modified form of the Church. I am quite convinced that many of the old forms and structures have outlived their day and that one of the most serious obstacles to the experience of the Christian faith is the perpetuation of these stereotypes. So the institutional form of the church easily becomes more of a hiding place from the realities than providing opportunities for the nurture and growth of Christian persons.

This is precisely the "problem" here. It is not a "political" problem. I am sure I can hold on by reducing it all to the least common denominator of interest and willingness to face the implications of the Christian faith. The heart of this church is quite united in a willingness to go along, provided the major emphasis is achieving an over-all consensus based on the lowest common denominator of understanding, interest and commitment.

My own conviction is that priorities might well be reversed in a new church. Instead of primary emphasis on the "new unit" and the preacher's evangelism "getting in new members," the first concern might well be the cultivation and nurture of a community of faith and understanding and a commitment to the mission of the Church. Then there is reason for building "a new unit," there is a fellowship seeking others into which new members are received and a mission to which they become committed. Instead of building the institution first and seeking support for it, my primary purpose is to serve as the agent for calling a Church into being and then helping devise the needed forms and structures to fill the need.

Here I am speaking of creativeness in worship and in the development of spiritual life such as through "small groups" as well as creativeness in Christian education (Bible study, development of curriculum, Christian education for adults, youth and children).

This, to me, is the excitement and possibility of the "new situation." Of course, the same process can be encouraged in the established church, and I am open to that where there is genuine openness and freedom to move in new directions, but I am not cut out to be the caretaker, preserver, or promoter of institutional forms, especially where those forms have little correspondence to the nature of the Church, or authentic dimensions of the Christian faith.

The Church in our time is in for som radical changes to match the changes the world and I am quite in earnest abou being part of such a creative process. appears to me that this kind of thing going to have to occur at certain vit points if the whole body of the Church to find its way toward a new stance an posture in the world.

. . . I have attempted this summary c my position to indicate my complet readiness to follow through on any inter esting situation and also to suggest tha any move will require some real assur ances of the above possibilities.

. . . My appreciation and thanks fo your interest.

TOWARD THE BREAKING POINT

[To all appearances, at least as reveale in the minutes of the official boards, thing returned to "normal" during the summe months. The boards and committees wen ahead with their work in preparation fo the fall. Some attempts were made to il luminate the difficulties of the churc through drawing in assistance from th Ecumenical Institute. Informal conversa tions and efforts to communicate and cre ate better understanding went on acros the lines of leadership and opposition There is no official record of meetings o the groups opposed to the ministerial lead ership during the summer and into th early autumn, but doubtless such meet ings did take place, for a petition callin for a church meeting to request the resig nations of the two ministers, Dudley an Stoner, was circulated and signed by sev enty-four members of the church, and th Church Clerk duly issued a call for such meeting on a notice dated October 22 1965.

A few days later the church newslette announced the cancellation for plans fo the celebration of the seventy-fifth anni

rsary of the church which was to be held
ovember 21. It declared:]

"The call for a Congregational meeting
request the dismissal of our present pas-
rate, boards and church program is com-
etely incompatible with reverence for
e past, pride of achievement, joy in fel-
wship or renewal for the future. Because
this, it would be a travesty on our
unders and the community of Elmhurst
celebrate anything at this time."

[The Board Chairman immediately
)ctober 25) issued a call for a broader
urpose for the meeting to be held on No-
:mber 7—namely, for "A vote of confi-
nce in (1) the present church program,
) members of the official boards and (3)
inisterial staff"—holding that the call for
e special meeting had been issued with-
t consultation of the Moderator and the
hurch Council and without prior notice
the ministers. Members of the peti-
ning group responded, indicating that
e petition was not a complete "surprise"
the church leadership, that consulta-
n had been held, and that opportunity
d been given for constructive action in
e few days before the petition was
ally delivered to the Church Clerk.
Meanwhile, students at Elmhurst Col-
ze circulated a petition in support of the
inisterial leadership, and this petition,
zned by nearly one hundred students,
as addressed to the Chairman of the
oard of Trustees and to the membership
the church. A letter written by the
outh Council, approved by a vote of
xty-four to seven of the high-school
outh in support of the work of the
outh minister, Mr. Stoner, was circu-
ted by the Diaconate. The Diaconate it-
lf passed a motion requesting its chair-
an to read the report of the Special
iaconate Committee compiled the pre-
ous spring to the congregation on Sun-

day, October 31. The conclusion of this report was that the charges against the ministerial leadership were "not valid reasons
for dismissal" and that the "program and
ministers deserve a vote of confidence."
At this same special meeting of the Diaconate, motions were passed to ask the "opposition" "what specific plans they have
for the continuance of the church" and to
make a report "on the financial support
given in 1962 and 1965 by signers of the
petition" calling for the special church
meeting.

The study of the financial support of
the church by the dissident members
showed that the group had substantially
lowered its support since 1962. From an
average pledge of $166, the figure had
been reduced to $130. The pledges of the
forty-two persons under study were approximately equal to those of four persons
who had indicated they would withdraw
if the ministers were to be discharged.
Further evidence was produced to the effect that three staff members had pledged
nearly half as much to the ongoing work
of the church as the total group of forty-
two families who were signers of the petition. It was disclosed that the pledges for
the current year represented the highest
dollar income in the history of the church.

The special congregational meeting was
held Sunday, November 7, 1965, as called
for by the notice of the Church Clerk. The
assembly was notified that the first call
for the special meeting, by the petitioners,
had priority over the enlarged call issued
by the Board Chairman. The meeting
then heard the motion to limit debate.
This motion was defeated. There followed
the motion to eliminate all debate. This
motion was passed by a vote of 313 to 124.
The balloting on the question of the resignation of the ministerial staff then took
place, with the results reported at the very
beginning of this case study.]

COMMENTARY

[The Editor asked two participants in the Elmhurst Church crisis to review the pr ceding case study and to indicate (1) what needs to be added to make the story more adequa or valid and (2), in retrospect, what could have been done, if anything, to bring about reconciliation of the difficulties and to prevent the move toward an open break within t church. Their responses follow.

The editor also asked the late Fred Hoskins, former minister of the General Council the Congregational churches and later co-president of the United Church of Christ ar Professor of the Parish Ministry at the Seminary, for his reflections. Dr. Hoskins dictat his comments just before his death. He was at the time of his death minister of the Gard City Community Church.]

MR. ROBERT CROWELL:

Please accept my apology for the delay in providing you with my reaction and comments concerning the material which you forwarded to me for review.

I have carefully studied the proposed article and should like to offer the following general comments:

1. In my opinion, the case study is well written in a manner consistent with the spirit and purpose of the study as set forth on page 2.
2. I recognize and can vouch for the various source documents which were used and identified in the study as being copies of official correspondence and minutes of various church meetings.
3. The chronological sequence of events involved in the situation is accurately portrayed.

As stated in item 2, I could readily identify all the source documents referred to; however, there were several other pieces of correspondence which, in my opinion, also had a significant bearing on the outcome of the situation. Since you made no reference to these documents, I thought perhaps that they may not have been included in your total file. I have taken the liberty of providing you with copies of these documents with the thought that they may be of some value to you.

Subsequent events have occurred whi you may wish to follow up in order complete the total case study. I am refe ring specifically to:

1. An article written by Mr. Ron Goetz, professor of religion at Elmhurst Cc lege, which appeared in the Marc 1966, issue of the *Renewal* magazin
2. The submission to the publisher of tl *Renewal* magazine of a "rebuttal" a ticle by Oscar Bowman, minist of Christian education at Bethar Church, Chicago.
3. A request from the First Congreg tional Church of Elmhurst throug proper church channels to the Nort east Conference of the United Churc of Christ for a clarification and a co rection of inaccuracies in Mr. Goetz article.

I believe that a careful review of two the above-mentioned articles would pr vide further insight into some of the bas problems underlying the total situatio

Since our first conversation concernir this proposed case study, I have a tempted to assess in retrospect all that h happened with the objective of trying determine, at least to my own satisfactio whether there might have been some oth constructive way in which the total situ tion could have been handled that woul

ve avoided the ultimate action that re-
lted. After much soul-searching, I am
mly convinced that the personalities of
e individuals primarily involved in the
:uation played a major role in the devel-
oment of negative attitudes on the part
a substantial segment of the congrega-
on. Because of either the inability or the
willingness of such individuals to bring
oout any change in their personal rela-
onships with dissenting elements of the
ongregation, I do not honestly believe
at any amount of hindsight would have
ought about any other result than that
hich finally occurred.

As a closing comment, I must stress
;ain that all the opinions and expressions
ontained in this communication repre-
nt only the personal views of one indi-
dual layman and member of the First
ongregational Church of Elmhurst. In
o way should they be construed or inter-
eted as representing any views or opin-
ns or positions of any of the official
urch boards, committees, and so forth.
hey are offered for the same reasons and
the same spirit as those you have cred-
ed with motivating the development of
is case study.

[Mr. Crowell refers to a document
gned by the chairmen of the various
oards, dated October 25, 1965, indicating
at the call of the special church meeting
r November 7 had been issued without
onsulting the Moderator and the Church
ouncil, and without prior notice to the
inisters, and the response signed by the
hairman of the Board of Trustees taking
e position that the call for the special
eeting "was not a complete surprise to
l factions." He also inclosed copies of a
ocument, dated April 6, 1965, and ad-
ressed to the Chairman of the Board of
eacons, that requested the presentation
 a constructive proposal by the "opposi-
on group" to the Church Council and of
letter from the Chairman of the Board

of Deacons, dated November 1, 1965, and
addressed to Mr. Crowell himself, that
inquired "as to what specific plans the
group you represent may have for the continuance of our church" and suggested the
difficulties that would be involved should
the vote "go against the ministers."—
EDITOR.]

DR. JOHN W. HANNI:

Space will not allow an analysis or detailed commentary. I will present my personal view.

Elmhurst is a typical middle-class suburb with a superabundance of organizations designated service, youth, philan-
thropic, and educational. Many owe their
origins in the past to important cultural
needs, but present "programs" are relics,
directed at the top by a professional core
which maintains the established order to
which the membership adapts in spite of
its precious local autonomy. The "cause"
is supported by social activities which are
vigorously publicized, often with subtle
suggestions of eliteness. The typical annual dinner dance entails a cash flow of
thousands of dollars, and 1 per cent of the
proceeds is ceremoniously presented to
maintain the hierarchy and to fund the
"cause." One can but conclude that these
organizations endure because suburban
man is lonely and alienated from his
neighbor. He will join damn near anything
which provides even an illusion of meaningful contact. Our church was a part of
that culture—so much a part as to have
lost any judgmental function with respect
to its milieu.

Local church historians recall that a
senior minister with twenty-five years'
tenure was discharged about 1945 amid a
fog of obscure issues and bewilderment.
His successor lasted seventeen years. An
assistant was fired, but the senior minister
was permitted to resign in a retrospec-
tively obvious maneuver to keep peace

29

and a semblance of unity in the institution. This minister was a stern, fair, pious, conscientious man, aware of everything from worship committee to heating plant, and a major building program was completed under his paternalistic guidance. The social activities of the church were thriving. The church was accorded an aristocratic aura conferred on anything old, first, unique, or original, as it had been the first liberal Protestant body in town. Policy and power resided predominantly with the Trustees, and the Church Council existed in name only. The Trustees instituted a second building program but aborted it, sensing a lack of congregational support. Within two or three years came the permitted resignation mentioned above. Again, few, if any, members had clear notions of the controversial issues. There were a pro-clergy group, an anti-clergy group, and a much larger number of people who were merely member-spectators.

With the new leadership in 1962, the illusion of unity nourished our naïve hope. New programs took root, especially in the areas of worship and Christian education. A "core" group responded with active participation, supported by several "small groups." Theological literacy increased, and a beginning awareness of the church's relevance to the world developed. Simultaneously there was a shift of power and policy-making from the Trustees to the activated Church Council. The laity was in some measure asserting itself and in some measure reacting to prodding by staff. These changes resulted in a mixture of joy, dialogue, resistance, and polarization of the fellowship into core and periphery.

At this historical point, the only possibility of reconciliation was a clearer definition of the reciprocal functions of lay and ordained. The democratic process functions creatively when openness and flexi-bility permit confrontation of traditi
and change, caution and boldness, ritu
and spontaneity. The brittleness of our i
stitutional structure dictated that uni
and function were dependent on t
strength of the ordained (a kind of p
pacy) supported by an authoritarian co
sistory (the Trustees). The laity could n
be true to its mechanical commitment
the democratic process. The church co
stitution was a feeble instrument. It fail
to provide a structure that could endu
tension and dissent. The ministerial st
at this point was most vulnerable, havir
the dismal choice of peacemaking or a
vocacy, recognizing that dismissal cou
occur "at any time by a majority vote a
meeting duly called for the purpose."
short, the minister was the constitutio
ally sanctioned scapegoat, whose dismiss
would theoretically heal any breach.
careful reading of Mr. Anderson's lett
will reveal a subtle shift from notions
collective (lay) responsibility to the sing
lar ministerial performance (e.g., "o
ministry to all the world," followed l
"Does he [minister] seek out his people?"

Democratic polity has proved histo
cally that it can serve effectively in tl
Body of Christ, but it must be discipline
informed, and responsible, especially as
confronts the urbanized, secular world.
is my conclusion that what has happene
in this church is only slightly regrettabl
We who have left feel that we have bee
given an exciting opportunity for creati
churchmanship, which is already und
way. Those who remain, facing a challen
to survival, must evaluate and change.
look forward to a time when the two co
gregations will collaborate in the work
Jesus Christ in the world.

FRED HOSKINS:

I wonder if this study of the Elmhur
Church can, indeed, be an objective ar
adequate presentation? I wonder becaus

30

it is objective and adequate, God help all if we have so far fallen into confusion out our identity as the church of Jesus rist.

Let it be said at once that no respon- le Christian can read the Elmhurst ory and self-righteously point the finger judgment. Notwithstanding, it is surely ad, sad story. For seventy-five years a dy of wonderful men, women, and ung people naming themselves the rst Congregational Church gladly have d that theirs was the whole church of rist particularized in their fellowship in eir place. Yet the seventy-fifth anniver- ry of the gathering of the church could t be recognized because the dissension as so great that none could remember ything to celebrate. Here is sheer trag- y. Covenant, truth, love, duty, mission ve fallen, and startling is the sound of e fracturing.

The saddest thing of all is that the Elm- rst tragedy is not a unique or even common phenomenon. I wonder if I uld not readily substitute percentages numbers, blanks for some names and aces, and find that members of many a urch about the land would easily believe e story a plausible description of their n. We have here word of a great sick- ss that is abroad. Elmhurst is not strick- with a different disease. The singularity the Elmhurst experience mostly is in e degree of advancement of the afflic- on.

I wonder why we have not learned tter how to engage in Christian contro- rsy? Always the church has contro- rted matters of self-understanding, th, life, and work. It is a reasonable ess that it always will. Probably con- oversy under the discipline of Christian rvanthood is a very effective way of un- vering further truth. In any event, min- ers and laity surely must study how to rther their mutual understanding of the nature and task of the church through the creative use of controversy. The goal is not to make of the church an insignificant unicellular ameba but a body of diversities unified by loyalty to Christ, service to God, and submission to the Holy Spirit's guidance.

Assuming the objectivity and adequacy of the study of the Elmhurst Church, I wonder:

1. At the lack of evidence that the church was aware of *sin*—was confessing sin and seek- ing forgiveness from God and one another.

2. At the lack of evidence that the church was wrestling in *prayer*. Does the church in our day imagine that it can resolve conflict, per- ceive truth, creatively capture values in variant perspectives of its members, discern and respond to God's will for it, outside of and aside from prayer—hard, persistent, and confident?

3. At the lack of evidence that the church was seeking resolution of its identity crisis by reference to the fellowship of the *sister churches* for counsel and guidance. No local church is an end in itself. Its successes, fail- ures, and problems are the concern and the responsibility of the whole church. The counsel, encouragement, mutual correction, and prayers of the sister churches are indis- pensable to the fullest self-understanding and proper ministry of every local church, whatever the denomination. Are not the sister churches and the fellow ministers al- most as culpable as the Elmhurst Church itself?

4. At the lack of evidence that the church was seeking to determine its identity with con- stant reference to the light and the author- ity of the *Holy Scriptures*. Every local church reads bits of the Bible in formal worship services. Does it, however, really search the scriptures for God's Word re- garding its nature, purpose, work, and style of life? Power groups and authority figures may not be convincing, however eloquent, simply by putting finger to forehead and intuiting answers to very complicated ques- tions.

31

5. At the lack of evidence that the church was seeking to agree upon what it is and how it is to live by constant reference to the authority of *Christ*. Doctrinaire positions, whether rooted in nostalgia, cultural assumptions, sophisticated theologizing, or inertia, simply must be held under the judging, the informing, and the transforming presence and mind of Christ.

I wonder if everyone who reads Elmhurst story does not immedia identify with one or another party to controversy. To himself does he not "Thou art the man?" His question is "What would I have said or done h been there?" His question is, "What a doing in my church wherein there is same identity crisis?"

A STYLE OF MINISTRY

[*Every churchman, whether he be ordained or not, has his own style of ministry, if he t the Christian life seriously. What style of ministry, one may wonder, was William D ley's? In 1964, in our special issue entitled "Ministry with Men," we published one man's report of his experience under Mr. Dudley's ministry in an Ohio congregation. reprint that account for what light it may shed on the story of the difficulties in the Elmh Church.*]

I think you do make a decision; you reach a point where you have to decide whether you wish to go all the way or whether you wish to back off. You do approach such a point, and you're never going to be the same again. You can't turn your back on it. But I also think that you have to keep making that decision.

This process of renewal, redemption, whatever you want to call it, is an ongoing thing during which you have many setbacks, failures, disbeliefs to live with. But the important thing is that, having made that decision, having experienced any part of its consequences, you can never go back. You may be afraid. You may see the price. You try, but you can't back off.

But this pastor, whom I was beginning by now to know as a person, achieved much of what he did achieve, I think, simply because of his personal deep-seated integrity and involvement.

This was true not only in what he said in the pulpit but in every contact one had with the man. You knew that he was struggling with something, and that he saw, in a sense, a great truth. All he was asking us to do really was to get into this thing with him and start considering some of the things that are basic rather than the

superficial piety and moralistic sta that Christians have held gener through the years.

He would say things like, "I don't c whether you believe in the physical re rection or not; the important thing i Christ confronting you or not? Is he al Does this have any meaning to you? D it raise any questions?"

What I'm trying to get at is the rat sudden onslaught of glimmerings and derstandings that all hit me about same time. And this I regard as a for tive period. You're considered some k of nut if you attempt to take some kin stand from a Christian viewpoint. Tod some years later—I'm not trying to t credit for anything, but it's true— whole character of our conversations work has changed. I find that there others who feel as I do.

This whole business of all of us runn around the country and talking is so thing most ministers just couldn't all Our pastor got a bear by the tail th and he never knew what any of us going to say. And yet he never sai word. He knew we were wrong m times, but his understanding of this volvement in the process of growth

32

ʰed him to see that we had to go through
s and that we might fail on things. But
thought that we ought to be allowed to
 what we felt.

I think the Bible class as such assumed
nificance largely as a result of my pre-
ʔus experience in the so-called cell
ʔups. I had been aware that there was a
ɔle class but had no particular interest
it, because, being biblically illiterate, as
ɛ saying goes, I could conceive of noth-
; but my previous experience in church
ʔool as a child. What could I get out of
ble study other than perhaps learning
torically about the life of Jesus, for ex-
ɪple, and perhaps rememorizing the
ɔks of the Bible? And this really had no
rticular meaning to me.

I had no understanding that the Bible
ʊld speak to me where I am now, in my
ɪe, and with reference to myself as a
rson and to my personal problems and
ɣ relationship to the rest of the world.
For the first time, in the group studying
ɔsdick, I began to see that the Christian
ɔspel did have something to say not only
me but to the world. The tendency is, I
ɪnk, for the uninitiated to regard the
urch as something set apart from the
ɔrld. And here was Fosdick seeking to
ate me to the whole process of relating
ɛ church to the world. This had a tre-
ɛndous impact.

It was about this time that we first un-
rtook the study of Paul's epistle to the
urch in Rome. And this was a real
ɔcker, a real inspiration. I can't even
ɡin to describe the over-all effect that it
d on me at the time and has had ever
ɪce. This, for the first time, really
ened up the whole spectrum of what's
ʋolved in Paul's concept of justification
 faith, for example. This was nothing
w; I'd always heard it, but I never un-
rstood it. Not to say that I do even now,
course, but. . . .

It came to have a personal meaning to
ɛ—that I was involved in something of

this same process that brought about
Paul's conversion. He was an adult convert. I'm an adult convert really, and yet
in a much smaller sense. As I came to
know Paul, not just his writings—you see,
involved in this Bible class was some
study of Paul, the man—all of this I was
able to relate directly to myself.

Well, this was a big part of the genius of
the pastor, as far as I was concerned. He
never was concerned too much about anything other than asking the question,
"What does this say to me, to all of us,
now, not two thousand years ago when it
was written?"

And he would constantly use as illus-
trative material pages from contemporary
magazines and news stories, political
events, economic situations, and the whole
business. I was able to relate the whole
thing to the situation that we find ourselves in today. This, I'm sure, was the
big breakthrough as far as my intellectual
understanding was concerned. My great
fear, as I've already said, is that that is
about as far as it has gone.

Here was a man who was not just talking at us or laying the thing out in front of
us saying, "This is what you ought to be
doing; these are the questions you ought
to be asking." Certainly he was saying
this, but he was himself constantly involved to the extent that you were always
aware that he himself was really struggling with these things. In his sermons, for
example, he wasn't just reading a carefully prepared sermon, or one carefully
memorized, or one that he had reduced to
notes. You could watch the man himself
struggling there in the pulpit.

I can recall many times when we would
be off somewhere, and a new aspect of
something that we'd been struggling with
—some new angle, some new idea, some
new insight—would come to him, something that perhaps he hadn't been able to
work out in his mind yet. He would throw
this out, and we'd kick it around, and all

of us would struggle with it, and the next Sunday there'd be a sermon on it. He might have had a sermon topic picked for that Sunday, but it would go out the window, and he would preach on this matter that was freshest in his mind.

In the whole process of this ministry his understanding grew and his concept of the church changed. He was not the same man when he left that he was two or three short years before that, and I hope the same can be said for me and for all the rest of us. I hope we grew, but I'm sure that none of us grew quite as much as he did.

And constantly there was the feeling of one thing now, and another day, another thing—another piece of the picture falling into place, so to speak; things that perhaps subconsciously you had been concerned about now coming to the fore and assuming their proper perspective.

This whole idea of the void in my life was something that I had recognized but had no idea that the answer lay in the church or had anything to do with religion, because I never knew that you could identify anything that had to do with religion with your life.

And any problems that I ever had—specific problems in terms of my relationship with my wife or my job or anything in that context—never did I dream that any of them might have to do with anything that the church might have to say.

This whole matter of personal relationships is a tremendously complex thing. All of us have built walls around ourselves. I had never been really involved with other people, never really known others, even those within my own family up until that time.

One of the things that was most revelatory at the beginning and since to me in this association, within our fellowship and without it, has been that I could—with some people, and it's been an increasing number—be myself and know that they were being themselves.

Now this is not one-hundred per cent

true. I don't think we ever completely reveal ourselves to anyone; but, at least, there was and is a feeling among many of us that we can "put our worst foot forward," so to speak.

And this, of course, is what we've come to see as a part of the real meaning of Christian education for our young people. This is basic to the whole matrix (that's the word we've been using) of our experience. And, if this kind of interpersonal relationship doesn't exist, nothing very significant can happen—at least, I don't think it can.

For example, when my son was in the hospital, we turned around, and there were three of our friends from the church. We didn't even know that they knew about it. There wasn't anything that they could do, but they did more than they could ever know or realize just by being there.

I don't know what I can say, except that it has helped me immensely to accept myself for what I am. And this is really a tough one. I don't know how it comes about other than to say that it does happen within some of these small groups over a period of time. It does involve some sense that we're all sons of God and that we're therefore necessarily closely related to one another. If we can just begin to see it, to begin to understand it, then what affects you affects me. This could become sloppy, sentimental-sounding stuff, I'm afraid, but I very definitely have the feeling that there are a number of people that I could call on at any time for any reason and I would hope that I'd be able to respond to such a call myself.

We want things to happen on our terms and on some kind of timetable that we set up, without realizing that this force that we don't understand and which we relate to and set up in our image—this God that we somehow believe but can't really know is real—is constantly working in our society in ways that we don't understand and can't possibly comprehend.

Part II
Contemporary Comment

From Renewal Magazine - March, 1966

The Power of Negative Action

By RON GOETZ

When the minister of a church gets "the axe," people usually try to pre-vent the matter from being published. Even though the reasons for the firing had nothing to do with the minister's morals or his competency, propriety requires that the news be passed through the usual channels of gossip. But whenever possible, public discussion must be avoided. This is done for the mutual protection of the church and the minister himself.

A few months ago, the minister of my church, the Rev. William Dudley, was voted out of his job. While it is usually neither courteous nor useful to discuss such an event in a public forum like a church journal, there are implications in this matter which are too significant to let die on the altar of ecclesiastical tranquility.

Specifically, I refer to the eruption which occurred in Elmhurst, Illinois when the First Congregational Church voted to require the resignation of its ministers. The ouster occurred in a public meeting last November 7th and it was a close vote. Of the members present, 245 voted for Mr. Dudley's resignation while 223 voted to retain him. The Rev. Donald Stoner, minister of Christian Education, "won" his contest, but by a very close vote. The two men had made it clear that since they had worked together on a program that both believed in, they would stay or go together. Faithful to this commitment, Mr. Stoner served notice of his own resignation immediately following the vote.

The First Congregational Church of Elmhurst was at one time, and perhaps is still, the prestige church of this well-to-do suburb. It was the church where the "best people" of the town could be met. It was the center of many social functions. It was the building in which middle class existence could receive its final gilding, the place where God could be required to sanctify all that we are and do. Elements were present in this institution which are typical of the suburban church at its theologically superficial, socially reactionary, idolatrous worst. It was a plump target for the most bitter irony and sarcasm. The following list is an actual reproduction of a rather typical former Lenten program for adults:

Lenten Program

Old Testament Characters	Exploring our Christian Concerns
Bowling	Agenda Group
Ceramics	Bait and Fly Casting
Puppets	Dramatics
Desire to Join the Church	Sqaure Dance Group

Some of the activities do have lenten relevance, i.e., they lead to greater self-discipline, which in turn allows us to bear the yoke of Christ with more steadfast dedication. The expert fly-caster, for example, gains remarkable control of hand and wrist and brilliantly coordinates these movements with his depth perception. Further, the stuffed and chemically preserved fish is a symbol of Christ for much of Christianity.

It is easy to tear the flesh from such a charade, but there is always the danger that we will ignore the fact that there are serious Christians trapped in these religious societies dedicated to such quaint posturings— Christians who are in the church in response to Christ's commands but who cannot find *any* church which is much better. The Elmhurst Congregational Church had such a remnant. This is why Mr. Dudley was called in the first place. Enough people had insisted that superficiality must come to an end and the church, badly split during former ministries, decided to give his ministry a try.

When Dudley and his staff took the reins of the church, they did not seek to destroy the numerous card clubs, ladies' guilds, self-improvement clinics, etc. Instead, they extended their efforts in other ways, especially in the creation of a number of small study groups dedicated to Christian learning and fellowship. An even greater split occurred, when many engaged in the new program testified that for the first time Christianity was making vital sense to them. Others grew angry at the ministerial neglect of functions which were the church's business from their point of view.

This situation gave rise to a prolonged guerilla action by those who felt themselves deprived of their church, while those who supported the new ministry joined various church boards and bade fair to become the new establishment. Compounding the animosity which ensued was the barrier of communication which seemed insurmountable. Many board meetings were torn apart by the inability of the dissenters to voice their objections and the inability of the program's supporters to lend a sympathetic ear. To add to the chaos, lurking in the background were various political and social questions. Dudley and staff were Democrats in a town that has never voted for a Democrat! This is one of the few northern counties where Goldwater won. Related to this was the race question: Dudley and staff didn't push politics, but on the race issue, they were firm and intransigent. Elmhurst is one of the few "lily-white" suburbs left, and Dudley rarely let this pass unnoticed.

In what was ostensibly an attempt to pinpoint objections to the new church program, several apparently well-meaning individuals decided to poll a segment of the congregation to determine precisely what their objections were, hoping that this would lead to their correction. What resulted was the total breakdown of all communication. The published list of complaints was circulated and now church-wide sniping at the ministry was apparently officially sanctioned.

This list of complaints represented the grievances of over 167 people. If a person had one complaint or twenty, they were duly listed under categories such as "Board of Christian Education" or "Board of Christian

Social Action," or "Sermons," or "Attitudes of Ministers," etc. Some objections were personal, relating to an individual's dislike of the various ministers. Some were trivial, showing displeasure over the use of modern art in the Christian Education curriculum. Some were unrelated to the present ministry, e.g., resentment of affiliation with the United Church of Christ. Many objected to the sermons, feeling they were incomprehensible or that they were too judgmental and not sufficiently "inspirational." Quite common was the feeling that communication had broken down.

Even the most tranquil of ministries would be threatened by asking a large part of the congregation to list their grievances—not their positive feelings—only their grievances.

Finally the church meeting was called in which a vote would be taken concerning the continuation of the ministry. The meeting was a disaster. People were, for the most part, ignorant of the issues, but tired of fighting. Hostility ran high. The Chicago Bear football game was on the radio at 1:00 P.M. and the meeting would cause the fans to miss the kick-off. Some showed up with portable transistors and ear plugs. Many had meals to prepare and dinner obligations. Nominal members who had attended rarely through the years, were probably uncomfortable in the strange environment. They had come only to vote Dudley out, knowing that a man who can't "keep the lid on" doesn't know his job. Then, because they desired to vote quickly and get out, the majority voted to cut off all debate. Dudley was not given a hearing and since he had anticipated debate on the matter, he had not preached on the question during his sermon. The fact that much of the lay leadership planned a mass exodus if the firing took place was never voiced. As the vote was taken, dissenters to the gag decision were shouted down and with remarkable dispatch, the ministry was ousted—all in time for traditional Sunday dinner to the accompaniment of the second half of the Bear game.

The meaning of this church's travail can best be described not by the events themselves, for they were confused, angry and frequently pointless, but in the light of what has happened since.

Immediately after the meeting, many of those who had been newly drawn to Jesus Christ through the ministry of Dudley and Stoner, came to a rather spontaneous decision—not that they would leave; this was a foregone conclusion.

What was newly and spontaneously realized, was a consensus that now seemed natural to them: the situation demanded a new beginning—a new church, but that it would be structured as something more than a Christian Country Club.

These people were not motivated primarily by bitterness, but as one person said, "I can not go back again." This was not an expression of anger, but of self-realization—an awareness of personal need of Christ's grace and presence if life is to have ultimate significance. The statement was a realization that we could scarcely hope to be found by Christ's Spirit in potlucks, women's clubs, card clubs, and all the other distractions which the church has erected to keep people from getting serious and choosing. The leaders of the exodus were not "young Turks" or radicals; they were solid Republicans—people who had constituted the leadership of the old church and who were angry now only at the years and years they had wasted. Some had been in the church for over thirty years.

In a sense, this whole dispute was pre-theological. There were and are few in the newly forming congregation (The Church of the New Covenant) who feel that they really have achieved full expression of their faith, or even of what the Church ought to be. But they realize that the Church and Christian faith are dependent on one another. They are not anti-ecclesiastical, though a certain anti-clericism runs high. While the new congregation is well aware of the dangers of institutionalism, they are not anti-institutional. All realize that any community of faith must have some structural framework.

Ultimately, the question is: To whom are the churches answerable? God or man? Will God be mocked forever? Can the Church as the "cheap grace" dispenser forever dangle the Bible, the sacraments, in front of people without someone, somewhere, somehow, grabbing hold and listening and hearing and calling out prophetically for reformation? This is what has begun to happen in Elmhurst, Illinois, a comparative spiritual wasteland, where social and political reaction runs high. I cannot but believe, though I tremble to suggest it, that a miracle of the Holy Spirit is being wrought.

The new congregation has decided fully on at least a few things: We want no building, now or in the future. We shall rent space as we now rent the chapel of Elmhurst College. The building we left had proved to be the master of the old congregation. If it is humanly possible, church buildings are to be dispensed with. If the fellowship breaks down, there should be as little brick and mortar as possible to hold a group together when the Spirit has fled. We realize this cannot be a universal course, but since it appears that we can do without property, we are overjoyed at the prospect.

Freed of this burden, we have decided that, at a bare minimum, one half of the church budget must go to missions outside the church. We shall encourage sacrificial giving, but the offerings will be for Christ's mission in the world.

Had there been any standards of membership at all in the old church, Dudley never would have been fired. It is a melancholy fact that while those who voted numbered less than 500, the total membership was over 1500. In a deep sense, we of the new congregation are grateful for the vote, for by driving us out of the First Congregational Church, they forced us into more radical thinking. However, the huge membership roll, kept high so as to drain as much money and stature out of its sheer number as is possible, is hopelessly inconsistent with any vision of Christian discipline.

When the decision was reached to explore the possibilities of a new church, the almost unanimous conclusion was to strive to write a church covenant which specifies a church discipline and which must be renewed by every member every year, as is done in the Church of Our Saviour in Washington, D.C.

We are frankly afraid of the whole matter of discipline, afraid for our comfort and afraid of legalism, but we are even more afraid to proceed without discipline. Thus, we have tried to develop non-legalistic specifications, requiring certain meaningful standards of ourselves in such matters as stewardship, worship and prayer, Christian education, conduct toward enemies, etc.

A number of our members do volunteer work of various types in the Chicago inner city. They shall continue and encourage others, but we are aware that serving the poor and dispossessed can be an excuse for irrelevance in our own community. We are increasingly concerned not only for our Chicago obligations, but for the equally critical crisis which faces us in the suburbs: *how to introduce our over-churched neighbors to Christ.*

I believe that the new congregation is remarkably sensitive theologically, but not yet really well-informed. While I know that something new is being done here, it grew, nevertheless, out of a ministry and preaching not radically novel, but seriously biblical. I pray God we continue this orientation, but I also am happy to see a greater determination for deeper theological study by the entire congregation. We are therefore attempting to re-face the problem of Christian education with an awareness that, generally, Christian education has failed. We need, and intend to explore, new avenues of inquiry which will involve children and adults alike, and which will relieve us of the burden of ignorant faith.

These are a few of the areas of renewal to which the Church of the New Covenant is quite vigorously addressing itself. What is being attempted here is a great tribute to the former ministers of the First Congregational Church. They sought no discord; they never wanted, nor did they expect, the struggle to lead to formation of a new congregation. What is of great significance is the fact that the ministers proclaimed the Word, without regard to their own futures, and the Word bore fruit.

It is my firm belief that what happened here is happening elsewhere and shall happen increasingly in the future. The church boom of the fifties disclosed the church's shameless promiscuity, its willingness to entertain as many as could be seduced into joining, irrespective of faith or commitment.

Certainly there are many in the ministry today who will continue to oil the waters and keep the churches peaceful and full at any price. The various denominations have enough organizational finesse to guarantee that no overwhelming upheaval will take place, but there is, I suspect, real ferment in the ranks. It stems from a hunger for a Christianity that makes a difference in one's life. How many laymen feel this way is hard to say. The proportion will differ according to congregation. But there are people who will respond to the preached Word with eagerness. This cannot help but breed division, for the majority in most congregations joined on terms far different than the Gospel provides.

41

It would be improper to denounce the average church-goer for his lack of dedication to Christ. It is profoundly unjust to criticize people for hypocrisy when they do a "culture dance" and call it Christianity. Many never would have joined the church had they expected judgment and challenge or the true peace which comes after the cross. How were they expected to know differently? Christian education has been a farce for years and the average excuse for a sermon, that pap which the ministry generally dispenses, serves nicely to hide the Biblical witness.

A minister who is an exception to the general run of oilers, as he comes into the "average" church, will be guilty of changing the rules in the middle of the game if he should preach Christ as the resurrected 20th century Lord. Such preaching must be done and there are those who will do it, but it cannot be done peacefully.

The old wine skins will not bear the living wine. Certainly the old denominational structures grow increasingly meaningless, as the struggle in the church is not over tradition and practice, but Christ and Mammon. Certainly this is a disturbing prospect. I do not commend party split or church dissension. Where peace is possible, disorder ought not be sought. However, turmoil will frequently follow a faithful ministry in the churches, constituted as they are today.

RON GOETZ is Instructor in Religion in the Department of Religion and Christian Education at Elmhurst College, Elmhurst, Illinois. He is a participating member of Church of the New Covenant.

From Renewal Magazine - August, 1966
Renewal Reactions

Editor's Note: The following statement was authorized in May, 1966, by the Council of First Congregational Church of Elmhurst in response to the article by Ron Goetz entitled THE POWER OF NEGATIVE ACTION which appeared in the March issue. In the interests of fair play and harboring a basic conviction that the pages of Renewal should be an open forum for the expression of opinions, we feel this statement must be shared with our readership. Such action illustrates The Power of Editorial Positivism.

If it be true that "there are implications in this matter (Mr. Dudley's dismissal) which are too significant to let die on the altar of ecclesiastical tranquility" it is equally true that there are allegations and implications in the article that are too questionable to be allowed to flourish unchallenged under the aegis of academic freedom. Herewith are quoted several of the allegations of facts, followed up in each instance with a statement of facts taken from the records of the church.

1. **Allegation.** "Elements were present in this institution which are typical of the suburban church at its theologically superficial, socially reactionary, idolatrous worst." As Exhibit A is given what is labelled as "a rather typical Lenten program for adults." The program: "Old Testament Characters, Bowling, Ceramics, Puppets, Desire to Join the Church, Exploring Our Christian Concerns, Agenda Group, Bait and Fly Casting, Dramatics, Square Dance Group."

Fact. This was the program for 1951 (fifteen years ago). To be properly understood it should be seen in the context of the total program initiated by the Board of Christian Education in 1949. According to its annual report to the congregation, "the purpose of this program is to provide opportunities in a growing church for closer fellowship and acquaintance in smaller interest groups, and to enlist more adults in active participation. Activities of an informal hobby type were instituted to show how religion may lift many aspects of life to a wholesome and high quality."

The annual report for 1954 included this paragraph: "It was agreed that this winter, while on-going interest groups would continue (such as bowling, volley ball, etc.) we would lay aside plans for other Congregational Adult Activities in order to concentrate on more specifically Lenten interests during that season of the church year." Ten years later, 1964 to be exact, a very complete and comprehensive program of Christian concerns was set up in a mimeographed booklet of thirteen pages.

2. **Allegation.** "Enough people had insisted that superficiality must come to an end and the church, badly split during former ministries, decided

to give his (Mr. Dudley's) ministry a try."

Fact. Neither the call extended to Mr. Dudley nor his letter of acceptance substantiate the allegation that the congregation wanted to experiment with a different kind of ministry. Such divisions as had existed had been largely overcome during the one year interim ministry of Mr. Oscar Bollman. It is noteworthy that Mr. Dudley was called by a unanimous vote of the members present at the meeting when the call was extended.

3.**Allegation.** "Several apparently well-meaning individuals decided to poll a segment of the congregation to determine precisely what their objections were, hoping this would lead to their correction."

Fact. The committee of four deacons, which did indeed endeavor to get at the objections, was not a self-appointed committee. It was appointed by the chairman of the Diaconate. The four members chosen were known for their non-partisan attitude. A total of 167 members appeared before the committee, another 22 communicated indirectly. All grievances were listed and classified as to substance, and a complete report was filed with the Diaconate and was made a matter of record.

4. **Allegation.** The meeting of November 7, 1965, is described as a "disaster." "People were, for the most part, ignorant of the issues, but tired of fighting." A Chicago Bear football game to be broadcast at 1 p.m. and Sunday dinner engagements are given as reasons for cutting off the debate.

Fact. The people were not ignorant of the issues, but "they were tired of fighting." This is attested to by the fact that at the very beginning of the meeting the congregation decided by an overwhelming majority that further discussion could serve no useful purpose. In contradistinction the vote to request Mr. Dudley's resignation was relatively close (245 to 223). Obviously, many of Mr. Dudley's supporters voted with his opponents on this motion. On the futility of further discussion there was widespread agreement. Clearly then, this vote was not a "gag decision," neither was it a parliamentary maneuver nor was it along partisan lines.

Concluding Statement. The sweeping indictments in the article to the effect that Elmhurst is "a comparative spiritual wasteland," that "Christian education has been a farce for years," that the average sermon is dismissed as "pap" and "hides the Biblical witness," and that by implication First Congregational Church of Elmhurst along with others is "a Christian Country Club"—are obviously statements of opinion, which—if they can be substantiated at all—can be substantiated only on a highly subjective basis. The committee is of the conviction that questions of opinion do not properly come within the scope of this reply.

Reflections on the Elmhurst Case

By CHARLES A. DAILEY

IT IS my earnest belief that every pastor and administrator can learn to draw forth the creative potential in any group, provided he learns to recognize, accept, and build upon the very human and sometimes immature needs in that group.

The essence of the problem of group tensions is the diverse set of goals for the congregation, and the apparent conflicts among these goals. Every group, including congregations and cliques within the congregation, seeks to maintain stability while moving ahead in a practical sense, and wants to do these two things (stay the same and yet achieve) while becoming what it can. The last of these three goals, growth, is so muted and subtle in the case of many groups that we will for the moment ignore it and primarily treat the conflicts arising between Stability and Achievement needs.

The essence of solution of any problem of group tensions is, of course, learning to identify the presence and cause of tensions early enough to resolve them; not merely to resolve tensions, but *to turn this unused energy to the purposes of achievement and growth.*

I will refer briefly here to the Elmhurst Church split a year or so ago, written up in the Chicago Theological Seminary *Register*.[1] This split crystallized during the tenure of a minister who lasted about three years after he attempted to change the structure and goals of a suburban church of around 500 adults. He was voted out in spite of the strong support of the most active board members of the church. Why? The opinion was offered by his opposition that his personality was so abrasive that his leaving was inevitable. The supporting faction said his policy was to create a church which stood for something and was not a mere local club.

These disagreements within the church appear at first glance more tragic than the similar difficulties in business and government. Our idealism and high hopes for the church render a church fight more intolerable. It is an element in American piety that there can be no happy warriors in church life. The Hymn-book of the Presbyterian Church is full of songs to work our courage up against the enemy and storms *outside*, but no songs to praise men *within* the congregation who are contending honestly and heartily with each other, to force a policy and a program. We sing for unity; we cannot find tongue to celebrate disunity. We do not admire the adversary system of finding truth.

On November 7, 1965, the congregation of this church met to request the resignation of the Pastor and an associate minister. The vote was 245 for the Pastor's resignation and 223 against.

He had come to this church late in 1961 following a major split in which two staff members were dismissed. Prior to this time the church, now over 75 years old, had served as a sort of social center in the Elmhurst community, and still had a number of groups of an interest type: bowling, ceramics, puppets, bait and fly casting, square dancing, and leather craft.

In 1958, the peak of membership and giving had been obtained. Since that time, membership had decreased, but pledges had increased. Fewer people were giving more. In 1964, the Board of Trustees, part of the "power structure" along with the Women's Fellowship, pointed to the decline of 17% in attendance during a time when the population of Elmhurst had increased 9%. The response of the Pastor to this analysis, which concerned a disinclination by the Trustees to adopt a 50% stewardship budget until attendance trends were reversed, was that it was not healthy to give to others only after paying our bills.

In August, 1964, the Church Council created a committee to consider the difficulties and dissatisfactions which seemed to be developing. During the next several months, various criticisms and defenses were offered. (The minutes seem to reflect the views of the Pastor's defenders almost completely.) The motives of the "power structure" are defined by the defense as an attempt to hold on to a "suburban Sunday morning social club."

At one point, the Pastor reflected, "... (we on the staff) see the situation as deteriorating until such time as there is a concerted and determined effort to meet the problem constructively. While we appear to have 'reached' quite a few individuals ... they do not represent the 'power structure' as it is represented by the Board of Trustees of the Women's Fellowship." The Pastor found it hard to characterize his opposition: they were not organized or articulate. He reaffirmed his unwillingness to be a "caretaker."

The Pastor pointed out that the decline in giving and attendance dated back to 1958, before his arrival, and was part of a complex national trend. In his diagnosis, he also pointed out that the congregation was aging, patterns had become set, and its original Community House function was no longer needed in a suburb which has developed many other social centers. Finally, that the church had been one demanding only institutional caretaking from the Minister.

Around January 1965, the Chairman of the Trustees had announced that the fund drive had not brought in enough money, and a hint was dropped that the people were "voting by pledge." The new deficit would reach nearly $7,800 in a budget of over $90,000.

Ninety-two families increased their giving to make up the deficit. A special committee talked to those withholding pledges for the first time and found eight families saying it was to protest, and twenty-four giving no reason. Another special committee now submitted its report of communication with 199 members and found about 31 different grievances in every area of church life including, among other things:

—that the social activities were being discouraged
—the program was being dictated by the national church
—the sermons were hard to understand, critical and offered little comfort to the congregation

A church meeting in May represented an attempt to review the areas of complaint and respond to them. We have no record of what happened in this meeting, but a few days later a statement was circulated, including remarks by the Moderator, Minister, and Chairman of the Diaconate. The Minister said he was agonized that he had evidently been unsuccessful, inadequate, and inarticulate. The Moderator said he was supposed to be impartial. The Chairman recognized the crisis, and asked everyone to stay with the church, admit his helplessness without the Holy Spirit, and reaffirm that with God all things are possible.

Other minutes of the official boards make it appear that things were back to normal on the surface after this. But in late summer, a call for a meeting to request the resignation of the two ministers was signed by 74 people. A special meeting was called by the Board Chairman for early November, for a "vote of confidence in the present church program, members of the official boards, and the ministerial staff." He rejected the call for an earlier meeting by the petitioners on the grounds that they had not consulted the Moderator or the Church Council.

At the November meeting, a motion was made to limit debate, defeated, and then a motion to eliminate all debate passed 313 to 124. Immediate balloting then favored resignation of the minister, and opposed resignation of the youth minister (who then announced that he would resign).

One observer of the situation cited the "personalities" involved as being primarily responsible for the crisis. Others noted the church as "part of a joiners milieu, so absorbed in antique, relic programs as to have lost any judgmental function." Dr. Fred Hoskins commented that "the Elmhurst tragedy is not a unique or even uncommon phenomenon . . . We have here word of a great sickness that is abroad . . . I wonder why we have not learned better how to engage in Christian controversy? Probably controversy under the discipline of Christian servanthood is a very effective way to uncovering further truth."

We now want to raise a series of questions about this case: in secular terms, what happened? what could have been done about it, at each of several successive points? what preventive policies should be proposed?

The congregation as a miniature culture

Custom and stability: a culture, such as that of a certain Colombian tribe, is obviously different from our own, is separated geographically from the outside world, speaks a different language, and resists change. We can view these cultural characteristics in Colombia as quaint or even attractive. We are offended to learn that our own home town is also a culture.

Any culture, as a system, will, however, defend itself. Outsiders are automatically regarded as alien and a threat to the order, in proportion to the power they wield. A new minister must become *acculturated* over a period of time.

Structure: every group, according to Eric Berne, has at least two boundaries: an external boundary (the outside world versus the inside world) and the internal boundary. If these are lost, we have only a formless rabble. This is not only empirically true, but may well be emotionally necessary if the members are to see a meaning in membership and an identity in the church.

Normally, in my observation, those at the top of any organization will miscalculate the degree and type of power which they have. The ministry has enormous power of some kinds, and this always implies a threatened loss of property, status, or security to *someone*.

In the Elmhurst case, the former upper echelon, the Board of Trustees, experienced a loss of status which few elites will normally permit, as perhaps this one did not. The attacks on its "territories" can come from outside the organization or from the inside. If attacks come from without, the normal response is to enhance internal unity, as would be the case for instance if the U.S. attacked mainland China. If the attacks come from within, unity is lost.

An implication of this analysis is that presumably the ministry attacked an entrenched status system during the first two years of its tenure, and was unable to recognize or extricate itself from this kind of family quarrel.

Time: the most effective industrial managers are normally those who make use of time without fighting it. The attempt to revise, within only two or three years, an entrenched social system which had built up precedents over 75 years, strikes one as exceptionally naive. In contrast, even with much greater power, an industrial executive will only very gradually succeed to power in a large corporation.

48

Time is on the side of administrators with long-range plans. Time normally opposes those who have basic goals framed in very short time spans. This does not mean that there is never an occasion for quick reform in an intolerable situation. Gradualism can sometimes mean paralysis. The administrator with a long-range plan is in a better position to act decisively and quickly than the administrator with a short-range plan. The short-range man only reacts nervously, and in contrast the long-range man can act decisively. I will observe, however, that I have found very few churches with a long-range plan—one outlining specific goals over a period of five to twenty years.

Reward and punishment: all cultures distribute reward to those who conform to the status and value systems, and punish those who do not, or who try to change it too fast. There is constant tension in most organizations over this process. The elite will usually under-estimate the amount of tension which normally or routinely exists because it is frightening and because they are hidden away from the frank expressions of the lower echelons.

In general, most reward and punishment seeks to maintain the *status quo* in any organization. The attempt to change the *status quo* therefore provokes tension. The art of doing this is more essentially the art of administration than is the bureaucratic art of maintaining the *status quo*. It is, therefore, well said that the management of change is closer to the definition of management than is the maintenance of routine. Leaders must lead. But they can expect a constant outpouring of punishment for this kind of leadership. As they receive this outpouring, they gauge its quality and amount, as a fundamental guide to knowing whether they are moving too fast or not.

Sense of strain: the individual expects, according to the fundamental theory of Homans, to find a balance between what he receives and what he gives. He receives a high status from the organization and therefore will feel a noblesse oblige. Or vice-versa, when the cost and reward are not balanced, he feels a sense of strain. When this goes on too long, health can be effected, or the person will leave. Anxiety is a cost. This congregation perhaps voted the ministry out to end the period of uncertainty. They were receiving so little gain in comparison to the worrying they were doing, they could not continue to endure the situation. To end the "cost" to themselves, they made the minister a scapegoat.

The above types of strain can be alleviated by patient negotiation and compromise. One type remains that appears to be existential. This is what Bales describes as two sequences of events which start from "opposite poles" in the life of a large scale social system, and which proceed in opposite directions. Adaptation to the outer world versus working for solidarity.

Growth and conflict: there is a third goal of organizational life, a higher order integration of the best values from the yearning for Stability and the drive for Achievement, and that is the aim of growth and self-realization. Growth is generated when the sense of strain (between Stability and Achievement) is expressed in creative directions. That is, when tension erupts not so much in interpersonal conflict and power struggles, but in terms of a new determination to unify the factions while moving ahead.

An organization becomes what it can be—and probably does this only through the constructive mobilization of the very considerable energy generated by the clash among the diverse factions. During wartime, the diverse factions are thought to work together constructively, and immediately with the "outbreak" of peace, they fight again, as happened between U.S. labor and management following World War II.

The worst sense of strain normally issues from the conflicts between brothers or those who are close. A sizeable proportion of murders are of spouses. The most atrocious wars are civil wars. An appreciation of this fact can arise only if we see that the normal condition is one of *temporary* peace within the organization.

Emotional bonds: any culture is held together by emotional bonds among persons in certain roles. In group tensions, these emotions show, *but they were there all the time*. This is perhaps the hardest lesson for the rational administrator to learn.

One of the things a person feels emotional about is his gains and losses, or his rewards and costs, to use the terminology developed earlier. The emotion felt by a man who is not receiving his proper rewards (as in status coin) is one of resentment, which he will express as a sense of injustice. I believe that in the Elmhurst case, the rewards the membership felt were missing were an affectionate bond with the minister. What frequency of pastoral calls were made? Was the due deference expressed toward the high status membership of the power elite? The closest the membership could get to expressing these deprivations was to say that the sermons made them feel uncomfortable, the minister was sarcastic, and the good old unity and family dinners were gone. In short, "you don't love us."

How can the administrator love the social structure? That is like loving the football stadium or the freeway. But if our earlier premise was correct, that the people by and large can most frequently unite on the defense of the *status quo*, it is fair to say, "Love me, love my power structure."

And this seems almost a ludicrous request, but we had best understand the significance of such emotional bonds. Fritz Redl describes this in a classic paper on Central Persons in groups. A group requires some form of energy in order to form, and this is provided by group emotions which find it convenient and appropriate to crystallize around the leader. Depending on the kind of group emotion present, different kinds of personalities can provide suitable leadership for a group.

In general, a new minister steps into a complex social system where the needs for leadership will rarely be uniform. If he "promotes" a leadership team which shares the kind of common emotion suited to his personality, he may gain a congenial "Cabinet" at the expense of depriving several factions of "representation." The fringe factions have no one to "identify with" or otherwise focus their emotions upon. The chances are that they will find or invent competing leaders. At Elmhurst, the inarticulate fringe groups crystallized emotionally upon a Villain, the Minister, and the common emotion was one of mistrust and fear of his intentions.

Rationality: the rational leadership should neither deny its own immature emotions, nor those of its opposition. How can the church, which has always known how sinful, parochial, and self-centered men are, without the Holy Spirit, pretend otherwise? Rational men are not those without emotions, but are men who admit them in self and other, and have learned to live in a constantly troubled world without losing their humanity. To become as little children means to retain our essential humanity.

Summary: in brief, we have discussed the following concepts of organizations and organizational dynamics:

stability: the organization yearns for stability and defends the *status quo.*

structure: one of the main things the organization defends is its structure.

Time: the sense of time and timing is the main distinction between the able and the inadequate manager of organizations.

reward and punishment: the organization keeps its shape and pushes toward goals by administering a complex system of rewards and punishments; one of the principal punishments is the sense of strain, of anxiety, which follows deviations.

strain: the organization structure, and the individual within it are subject to constant strain because of the inevitable imbalances between the different goals of the organization and the imbalance between the individuals' costs and rewards.

adaptation versus solidarity: every organization strives for goals and also strives to stay the same: these are in tension.

growth: the integration of these calls for the use of the tension or energy for becoming, for growing.

emotional bonds: the culture or organization is held together by emotional bonds, and it is also formed at the outset by use of certain emotions crystallized around the personality of one or more central persons; the manner in which this is done, and the emotions involved, will determine much of the character and purposes of the group.

immaturity: no one succeeds in growing out of these emotions, or in becoming totally mature.

rationality: rational leadership admits both its own emotions and those of its opposition without pretense.

In applying these concepts to the Elmhurst fight, I would say that the people of First Church had built a miniature culture, imbedded in precedents built up over a period of 75 years. A new leadership attempted to substitute too quickly a Church Council made up of persons whose goals for the church were more compatible with the goals of the minister. The strain of uncertainty, endured over a period of several years, became too much for the congregation, who sought unity by evicting the dissident leaders. The new leadership, unable to read the signs of discontent early enough, and unable to provide a means of relieving the fears of a minority or restoring communication to a haughty dispossessed elite had proved unable, therefore, to regain effective consensus.

Symptoms and first aid

Certain practical indicators of organizational unrest and symptoms of trouble are habitually watched by experienced administrators. Among them:

1. Attendance or revenue decline.
2. Withdrawal of support by influential "old families" and other "high status" groups.
3. Polarization of opinion and formation of factions who regularly take opposite views on all issues.
4. A persisting issue of abrasive quality.
5. Loss of communication with any faction or influential member.

Remedies—again speaking of the congregation as if it were only a secular organization like any other for the sake of exposition—fall into several broad classes

—renewal of contact with the vanishing sheep or the antagonists
—slowdown of too great a number of simultaneous or frightening innovations
—institution of joint long-range planning

It has *not* been suggested that all will be well if the festering issues are brought out into the open, or if the quarrelling factions have a confrontation. A sense of *timing* is more important than any other aspect in first aid. Open discussions and confrontations can be as ill-timed as any other form of first aid.

Strategies of conflict resolution

For the conflicts which have gone beyond "first aid" more basic therapy is indicated. Among the broad strategies normally used:

1. *Removal of conflict from the win-lose context:* If conflicts may only be resolved by someone *losing*, then the world will always be filled with Vietnams. Note: calling for a vote will often create this very win-lose context.

2. *Confining the conflict:* the natural history of conflicts is an expansion of the issue (little fires become conflagrations) and persons involved. Conflict-confining requires an early-*warning* system which is in continuous operation, and the settling of such grievances *early*.
3. *G.R.I.T.:* Professor Charles Osgood of the University of Illinois advocates a strategy he calls "graduated reciprocal reduction in tension," or GRIT for short. Each side gives. It is horse-trading not moralizing. Each side recognizes the dangers from conflict are greater than the dangers of being wrong.
4. *Bargaining and negotiation:* A whole style of administration is implied in this strategy. It is the style of management we find in the U.S. Senate and in Labor-Management relations. It is a difficult style for idealists, and requires very hard work and a strong stomach.
5. *Superordinate goals:* Some conflicts do not become resolved at all but become peripheral. They do this when two factions are confronted with an external problem they both accept and which they recognize they can only solve together.
6. *Mediation:* An external person, but without authority, can be called in to help both sides find a way to initiate some of the above strategies.
7. *Arbitration:* An external person with authority, accepted by both factions, can sometimes resolve a conflict.

Organization building

Clearly the best course of action is to build a strong enough organization to contain and solve conflicts. A strong organization normally has diversity, hence conflict. It normally pushes for goals, hence conflict with those who want to keep things as they are.

When the organization has learned to integrate the forces of stability with the forces toward change, it is strong. This may be done only by Pastors who recognize both human needs as legitimate.

How to build such an organization? Probably it has to teach itself to quarrel creatively. Pious organizations won't do this, and cannot achieve real strength. Pastors would do well to familiarize themselves with the language and tactics used in labor-management bargaining.

Constant sensitivity to grievances, prompt resolution of them, negotiation of every change with the persons who will feel affected by them, and joint planning—these are the normal cornerstones of labor-management relations and of international diplomacy as well.

Inevitability of tension

The conflicts are, however, inevitable in that every organization wants both to progress and to keep things the same. These are the *Yin* and *Yang* of organizational life.

Not least in the list of existential courses of conflict is the inevitability of rank. Hierarchies or ranks have been found to be characteristic of every society in the world. The Pastor's acceptance of the necessity of authority precedes his fitness to deal with its consequences. He will have the rank whether he accepts it or not. Protestantism has been a long time in recognizing this fact of life.

In closing, (1) I think of the congregational society as emotionally like a big juvenile or an adolescent. If you can like teenagers, you can find it possible to like the outrageous character of the congregation.

(2) True compassion can love even the immature and violent, and the best administrator is himself only a rational child.

(3) Structurally, every society is a network of status systems in constant tension. Peace is an illusion.

(4) Time is nonetheless on the side of the happy warrior, and of the administrator who has a long-range plan.

(5) The life of the large institution is dominated by the wrong persons largely because, as John Dewey says:

"Saints deliberate while burly sinners run the world."

Part III
Retrospective Comment 1974-75

Reflections Upon Church Renewal
1960 — 1974

By DONALD G. STONER

Books written in the field of religion over the past 15 years serve as a ready review of the issues and phases through which we have passed in church renewal. Beginning in 1960 George Webber in **God's Colony in Man's World**,[1] described the dire need for new wineskins to embody the traditional koinonia that exists to proclaim and witness to the gospel in the world.

Gibson Winter in 1961 analyzed the procession of Protestantism to suburbia in **The Suburban Captivity of the Church**,[2] its subsequent irrelevance to the desperate needs of the inner city, and the dim prospect of its renewal as directed to the non-residential sectors of life. He concluded "that the Church is deformed by the struggle to survive and reformed only as ministry and mission." In **A Private and Public Faith**,[3] William Stringfellow protested in 1962, against the self-serving religiosity that characterized much of contemporary religion. He wrote: "The American persuasion that religion has to do with religion and not the world is deeply appealing to the mentality of American people both within and outside the Church."

From the throes of the parish proper came such works as Robert Raines' **New Life In The Church**,[4] (1961), a manifesto calling for "koinonia groups" designed to change lives and to direct laity in a recovery of mission in the world. With a note of optimism he concluded, "The Holy Spirit is at work in power in our time. The dry bones are beginning to live again." The Church of the Saviour in Washington D.C. was described in Elizabeth O'Connor's **Call To Commitment**[5] (1963) as a model for the new forms of ministry i.e. coffeehouse, Potter's house workshop, that are required in our time.

In 1964 a book by Langdon Gilkey, with an awkward title but expounding sound theology appeared, **How The Church Can Minister To The World Without Losing Itself**.[6] Gilkey warned that the Church "can minister to the world, which is its task, without losing itself by becoming captive to the world, which is always its danger." Covering much of the same ground but with more practical approaches to evangelism were Colin Williams' two slender volumes **Where In The World** and **What In The World**.

The Grass Roots Church[8] (1965) was Stephen Rose's program for a total restructuring of the local church by having it engaged in the tasks of chaplaincy, teaching and abandonment as based on I Corinthians, Chapters 12 and 13.

The restructuring of the local church was abandoned as attention was focused on the need to relate the Church to the secular world as depicted by Harvey Cox in **The Secular City**[9] (1965). There followed in this wake of preoccupation with the secular, a number of authors who tried to "out secularize" each other. These ranged from Gabriel Vahanian's iconoclastic work, **The Death of God,**[10] an analysis of the dishabilitation of the Christian tradition and its replacement by bourgeois religiosity and a theology of immanentism to Thomas Altizer's arrogant and astounding thesis in **The Gospel of Christian Atheism**[11] (1966) i.e. "the message the Christian is now called to proclaim is the gospel, the good news of the death of God."

Meanwhile books were appearing that dealt with the ministers' identity, their relationship to parishioners, and in several instances reasons for their leaving the ministry. Among these were **Your Pastor's Problems: A Guide for Ministers and Laymen**[12] (1966) by William Hulme and **Neurotics in the Church**[13] (1963) by Robert St. Clair.

Then there appeared several "case studies" detailing the dynamics of local church conflicts. The CTS **Register**[14] (June 1966) was devoted to **The Local Church In Crisis**, detailing the "Elmhurst Story" from the various perspectives of those involved. **Rocking The Ark: Nine Case Studies in Process of Change,**[15] (1968) reflected differing church situations experiencing traumatic change. Arthur Herzog lent his zesty sociological analysis to First Church — Elmhurst and the signs of decline in organized religion in **The Church Trap**[16] (1968). Malcolm Boyd edited a "handbook" of what was happening in the "farthest out" segments of church life in **The Underground Church**[17] (1968).

Strategies to cope with the process of change and the management of conflict were offered as a key to resolving conflict and hastening the time of renewal. An example of such works was Charles Dailey's articles on conflict management in the CTS **Register**[18] (May 1969). A recent book of this type is **Church Fights: Managing Conflict in the Local Church**[19] (1973) by Leas and Kittlaus. It seems that some are making a living by being referees!

Beginning in the 1970's there came books that spoke of the revival of the Church. Findley Edge in **The Greening of the Church**[20] (1971) expressed hope in the future of the Church through emphasis on personal growth and spiritual life along with a continued need for evangelism and social action. In **Beyond Revolution: A Response to the Underground Church**[21] (1970) Thomas Oden seeks to answer why someone who believes and is concerned about the Church, should stay in it. He concludes: "Only the conserver who asks how the tradition can be relevantly renewed is faithful to the tradition." More recently Robert M. Brown in **Frontiers For The Church Today**[22] (1973) summarizes the many critics of the past 15 years and proceeds to offer a number of positive images for rethinking the task of the Church today.

A major theme that has emerged of late in the Church is what some refer to as "the new revival of the spiritual." Little did one suspect that beginning with the 70's there would be a resurgence of piety in the solemn assemblies; that "getting high" on Jesus would substitute for "tripping" with drugs for the young; that spirituality would be sought by adults in the most recent encounter groups or from the latest guru.

What has brought about this change of mood in the Church?

When it would appear that religion was in the forefront of working for social change, it was suddenly being looked to for stability to provide ballast in a society that had wearied of social causes. Security-seeking had won out over risk-taking. Dr. Carl Becker, in 1932, was correct in assessing the present mood when he wrote: "What the average man wants, much more than he wants the liberties we prize, is security; and he will support those who can and will give it to him."[23]

To a large extent this strong urge for stability and security is what accounts for the present mood in the Church and its quest for the spiritual. The spiritual represents for many that which is dependable, unchanging, trustworthy in a time that threatens instability, loss of direction and lack of values. For many it may appear as a "security blanket" rather than the nurturing of the inner depths of the soul that provides a basis for one's faith.

Granted that much contained in the present "spiritual revival" is self-centered and security seeking; can it be the occasion for a deeper, more thorough going time of spiritual renewal in the Church?

Dr. Martin Marty's counsel in **The Fire We Can Light**[24] is relevant here: "If the promise of American life is to be fulfilled, if freedom is to be extended and equality enjoyed, future moves will have to be made with some sense of regard for the love of ballast, the support of the formal system, or the drive for security. Such regard need not mean that people of vision simply must acquiesce to the world as it is. But they must have empathy for those who suffer in that world's mixture of slavery and freedom. True leaders will try to discuss the points at which people show discontent with the formal system or give signs that they might venture within the limits such a system permits."

This well summarizes the immense task before the churches where the strong inclination toward security may well thwart significant spiritual renewal.

When we were told that "religion was coming of age" and that secular man no longer had need of its spiritual ministrations, a new spiritual quest had been undertaken by many inside and outside the Church. To some even in the Church the spiritual life was thought to be unrecoverable or unredeemable. Yet this current spiritual quest has occurred and taken on many a diverse and often bizarre form. In order to satisfy their spiritual hunger people speak in tongues, join communes, worship the occult, or engage in meditation. On the whole the Church and the public have been receptive and relieved by this change of mood in the Church. Dr. Marty summarizes the reasons:

"America in the first third of the 70's was in a 'that's nice, don't fight' mood. By contrast to what had gone on in the violent 60's, there were many occasions for relief. Harassed elders . . . had never welcomed the communes, but when these were in the hands of gentle Pentecostalists, they shrugged, 'That's nice, don't fight.'"[25]

What is to be made of this change in the Church?

This spiritual quest is in part a reaction to a secular emphasis upon confidence in modern science and technology and a radical politic. While some have predicted that our society would become increasingly given over to what man can devise and control, the experiences of our time have proven that not all in life can be so contrived if human life is to remain humane and meaningful. There is more to life than one can provide on one's own terms. Secular man was supposed to be unconcerned about such things as meaning, mystery and mysticism. The current spiritual quest has proven otherwise.

In spite of this kind of reaction that has made for renewed interest in the spiritual, there is no denying that the Church in the recent past failed to provide sufficient spiritual nourishment.

The church leadership was preoccupied with what they considered to be the more urgent task of prophetic ministry in the world. The need however for meaning and power provided by spiritual preparation and fortitude has proven to be so necessary if persons are to be truly committed to ministering in the world.

Given the need and receptivity to spiritual renewal, the problem is one of providing suitable nurture of the soul without this becoming an end in itself. The great need is to convey the inter-relatedness of the life of the spirit (what is means to be "in Christ,") and ethical concern and action (what it means to be in and not of the world). Then and only then will the "whole counsel of God" be employed. An editor of **Reader's Digest** in responding to this frequent dichotomy in American Religion wrote:

"It seems as if the blacks, the kids, the women, the restless -- all the exciting people -- are doing religious things and talking about "soul" and "the spirit" while the church leadership talks about being organizational and worldly. Aren't you afraid that the two groups are going to pass each other in the aisle of the sanctuary . . ."[26]

How is one to assess the impact of this "spiritual revival" upon the churches?

The spiritual surge arrived in 1970 with the "pentecostals" and the "Jesus Movement." These groups and individuals have found acceptance in and had some impact upon the more conservative churches. Theologically they form a kinship reinforcing and giving vitality to what are the fastest growing churches in the United States.

In the declining mainline Protestant churches there are efforts to recover their forgotten heritage of pietism and evangelism. National agencies are providing workshops on the "faith crisis" and holding training sessions on "action evangelism." Increasingly, local congregations are seeking means to provide greater spiritual nourishment through more opportunities for Bible study and theological reflection.

The "identity crisis" experienced by the local church and the ministerial leadership is a second prevalent theme throughout the recent past and presently. The churches and their leadership were busy in the 50's constructing edifices to house expanding church memberships. The focus of ministry was principally upon congregational and family life.

In contrast, the mid 60's brought ministers into the streets with a few of their laity to protest treatment of blacks and United States involvement in South East Asia. The prophetic role took precedence over the priestly function of the minister without there being an adequate appreciation of the complementary relationship between the two.

The papers were quick to portray this tension. Editorially the *Chicago Sun Times* presented the case of First Congregational Church, Wilmette, Illinois. It read:

"The Church is wrestling with a dilemma that is confronting Christianity everywhere: What should be the Church's role in the world? Should its members and leaders actively participate in such causes as peace and civil rights? . . . Rev. Buckner Coe has resigned because of disagreement with his congregation over "race relations and peace and poverty." He said that some members thought he had 'gone too far' in advocacy of integrated housing but he himself believed he had not gone 'far enough.'" Getting at the heart of the matter was the response of a layman to his minister who was later voted out. "We get the idea that you're trying to change us."[27]

In seeking to change persons and congregations toward becoming more like the body of Christ, ministers experienced their own "crucifixion." Theologically this may well be the unavoidable and inevitable consequence of one's faithfulness to the gospel, for one cannot avoid the offense and scandal of the gospel. However, ministers were told that their leadership in the local church was politically naive, that they did not employ conflict management techniques, and that they possessed abrasive personalities.

Given these "hazards of the ministry" and the threats inherent in change, nevertheless some ministers do neglect what Dr. Marty calls 'precinct politics' in the Church. This involves an inadequate building of trust and support, concern and caring at the interpersonal level throughout the local congregation. A thorough ministry to the personal needs of the congregation can provide a strong basis for involving persons in concerns that reach beyond their immediate lives.

The minister of a church gains legitimate power by serving the needs of parishioners. There have been those who have decried or neglected this important pastoral function. This base provides the minister with role identity, dignity and value as a person in the eyes of the parishioners. The minister gains a base from which to extend his or her ministry to community and world needs.

The 70's appear to again be reflecting the strength and vitality of the local church. This period serves to provide the minister with a greater sense of being needed and valued. For the minister does bring a professional competency to a period in the Church that stresses individual growth, personal intimacy, and small group life. Consequently ministers are experiencing a greater sense of power and possibility as they look at themselves and their parishioners than was the case a few years earlier.

On the matter of health in the parishes, Dr. Marty reports ministers saying the following:

"There's a lot going on out there. The ecumenical and denominational forces do not know quite how to summarize it, and the media miss the story. But people have come through in amazing if quiet ways. Loyalty and dedication show up in surprising ways."

Marty adds: "These reports seem to contain the cynicism one heard when the ministers' main vision was one of congregational resistance to social change. These accounts are still being made at a time when the leaders are far from satisfied with their people's response to the Biblical prophetic note."

Local congregations are here to stay for quite some time. Those who predicted their demise and worked for alternative forms underestimated their staying power. Dr. Marty continues:

"We are too far into the cultural revolution to make the old forms really effective, but not far enough through it for the new forms to have emerged."[28]

In the meantime experimental and alternative church patterns have flowered and many withered. They have appeared mostly in the middle class suburbs, gathering the younger people who are restless, creative, and alienated from the conventional church. They have been viewed for the most part by the conventional church as a threat with there being little mutual sharing and exchange of ideas.

An urgent question becomes that of "how does one transmit a newly experienced sense of meaning and spiritual power to the established order?" Some feel that those engaged in church renewal should see themselves as **ad hoc** to the conventional church, as exiles from the homeland, and if things change, return. Dr. Robert McAfee Brown in **Frontiers for the Church Today** concurs in the idea that the renewal movement is necessarily provisional and critical, consequently persons involved must "stay related to the traditional churches even though the other ways of doing things may seem embarrassing."[29]

A third theme present in the social turbulence of the 60's and in the spiritual quest in the 70's is the need for coring or centering to occur in the Church. Too frequently those, who lay claim to being Christian, have been proven ineffectual, misdirected and distraught, because of a lack of a core or center out of which to minister. Without such a core or center the Christian can neither know who one is nor what one should be about in the Church, let alone in the world.

The core or center in Christianity is finding what is central to Christian faith and experience. It is a process, something not achieved; an intention toward which one moves, yet never finally reaches. In looking outward to mission in the world, the tendency was to neglect the nourishment of that which constitutes the core of Christian faith. The danger has been to lose the identity of oneself and the Church in ministering to the world.

This danger was prevalent in the Church when it came under the spell of the secular theologians who sent many in the church off on irrelevant quests for a basis of new life in the Church. Dr. Brown describes four dangers in this "secular seduction." 1.) The danger that an uncritical "theology of the secular" will end up being little more than a repetition of an earlier uncritical "culture-Protestantism." 2.) The danger of the loss of a sense of wonder of the mystery of human existance under the embrace of secularity. 3.) The danger that the Christian will be left historically and institutionally rootless. 4.) The need for a more dialectical approach to the secular. Thus, the shape and source of the church's life will come not from sustenance provided by the world but from the substance provided within its own life and tradition.[30]

Perhaps this is what Dr. Fred Hoskins was reminding us of when he added his critique to the Elmhurst case study.[31] He was challenging all those involved to ask where was the evidence that the authority of scripture and that of Christ were being sought after as a basis for being the Church. What, for instance, does it mean to be "in Christ" or to be "the body of Christ?"

The past 15 years in the Church has resulted in a lack of a core due to a certain theological faddishness which has prevented the Church from becoming a "centered people." The Church has been caught adrift in the world with only the marks of the world to provide it with sustenance and direction. Dr. George Webber, author of **God's Colony In Man's World,** reminded us in 1960 of the Church's need to find a center to provide it with direction and purpose in the world.

"If when we withdraw from our task in the world into the protection and renewing power of the colony, we bring the world with us, we may well be destroyed. I am under the impression that many American churches are bringing the Trojan horse into the midst of their common life . . . It is of necessity that we draw apart behind the walls of the colony, not because we hate the world or are seeking to rid ourselves of it, but precisely in order to have the strength, wisdom and courage to return to our calling in the midst of the world."[32]

This seeking of a center continues as the paramount task of the Church today, if its spiritual revival indeed be genuine and lasting. Then and only then, will the Church discover its true identity and experience continual renewal that will inform its mission in the world.

References

1 George Webber, **God's Colony in Man's World**, (Abingdon, 1960)
2 Gibson Winter, **The Suburban Captivity of the Churches**, P. 176, (Doubleday & Co., Inc., 1961)
3 William Stringfellow, **A Private and Public Faith**, P. 19, (William B. Erdmans Publishing Co., 1962)
4 Robert A. Raines, **New Life In The Church**, P. 145, (Harper & Row 1961)
5 Elizabeth O'Connor, **Call to Commitment** (Harper & Row, 1963)
6 Langdon Gilkey, **How The Church Can Minister to the World Without Losing Itself**, P. 1, (Harper & Row 1964)
7 Colin Williams, **Where In The World? and What In The World?** (Office of Publishing and Distributing National Council of Churches of Christ in the USA 1963)
8 Stephen Rose, **The Grass Roots Church**, (Holt, Rinehart & Winston, 1966)
9 Harvey Cox, **The Secular City**, (MacMillan, 1965)
10 Gabriel Vahanian, **The Death of God**, (George Braziller, 1961)
11 Thomas J. J. Altizer, **The Gospel of Christian Atheism**, (Westminster Press, 1966)
12 William E. Hulme, **Your Pastor's Problems**, (Doubleday & Co., 1966)
13 Robert James St. Clair, **Neurotics in the Church**, (Fleming H. Revell, 1963)
14 The Chicago Theological Seminary, **Register**, June 1966, Vol. LVI, No. 8.
15 Grace Ann Goodman, **Rocking The Ark** (Division of Evangelism, Board of National Missions, United Presbyterian Church, USA, 1968)
16 Arthur Herzog, **The Church Trap**, (The MacMillan Co., 1968)
17 Malcolm Boyd (ed), **The Underground Church**, (Sheed & Ward, 1968)
18 The Chicago Theological Seminary **Register**, May 1969, Vol. LIX, No. 4, "The Management of Conflict" and "Reflections on the Elmhurst Case," Charles A. Dailey.
19 Speed Leas and Paul Kittlaus, **Church Fights**, (Westminster Press, 1973)
20 Findley B. Edge, **The Greening of the Church** (Word Books, 1971)
21 Thomas C. Oden, **Beyond Revolution** (The Westminster Press, 1970)
22 Robert McAfee Brown, **Frontiers For the Church Today**, (Oxford University Press, 1973)
23 Quoted by Martin E. Marty in **The Fire We Can Light**, (Doubleday & Co., Inc., 1973) p. 23
24 **Ibid**, p. 24
25 **Ibid**, p. 56
26 **Ibid**, p. 61
27 **The Chicago Sun Times**
28 **Ibid**, p. 203
29 Robert M. Brown, **Frontiers For the Church Today**
30 **Ibid**, pp. 45-47
31 Chicago Theological Seminary **Register, op. cit.**
32 George Webber, **Op. cit.**, p. 143

Eight Years, Five Months, Seventeen Days

By WILLIAM H. DUDLEY

Except for moral lapses and unethical behavior ministers are almost never fired. They are eased out, advised to seek greener pastures, but rarely fired.

Such action in November 1965 by The First Congregational Church of Elmhurst, Illinois created an immediate financial and professional crisis for the fire-ee! Two daughters were in private colleges, one parent was financially dependent and there was a need for continuing income. Fortunately, during over a quarter of a century in the ministry we had never been permitted to develop anything more than a very modest scale of living!

During "the more successful years" the pastoral committees of more than a half dozen of the denominations "leading churches" had indicated interest in my ministry. Elmhurst was our deliberate choice because the committee (at least the articulate section) was quite explicit and certainly unique in acknowledging an urgent need for "renewal." The message was clear to me that this was to be the theme of my ministry in Elmhurst.

We had enjoyed such a pastorate in previous years. It was a church in which the people became involved. As the action developed groups of lay people responded to countless invitations from local churches, associations and state conferences to describe their experience — how it occurred, what it meant to them and how it changed them. I was thoroughly committed to this kind of ministry.

This is evident in a letter written by me to a state conference, which is quoted on pages 25 and 26 in "The Local Church in Crisis."

". . . I am not cut out to be the caretaker, preserver, or promoter of institutional forms, especially where those forms have little correspondence to the nature of the Church, or authentic dimensions of the Christian faith . . . The church is in for some radical changes to match the changes of the world and I am quite in earnest in being a part of such a creative process."

An anecdote enlarges on this point. On one occasion a group of our women were invited to an area meeting to lead a discussion on "Women's Role in the Church." I gave the keynote address followed by a short break before getting in to small group discussion. During the interim two of our women reported overhearing an interesting conversation in the ladies room. One lady enthusiastically exclaimed, "My, wasn't that a fine talk we just heard!" The other responded "Yah, the talk was all right, but I'd sure hate to have him for my minister!"

And that's the way it was in Elmhurst. While most of the official family were supportive (with the exception of some members of the Board of Trustees and some representatives of "fellowship groups"), when it came to counting noses the majority of the voting membership didn't accept that style of ministry. Incidentally, it is true I didn't recognize some of the people who were present for the vote and I'm not sure they knew me by sight. Some were reportedly ignorant of the identity of my associate also facing a vote for survival — which is to say these people were not red hot members, but they were voting members and that's what counted when the chips were down.

At any rate, we had known for some time we were in for it. Shortly after dismissal my wife and I organized a garage sale and unburdened ourselves of 95% of our household and personal possessions in order to prepare for what we may euphemistically call "a new mobile life style." A few months earlier my wife took a business school refresher course and found employment as a hedge against our anticipated loss of income. Several months before the firing I persuaded an associate on the church staff to seek shelter and he had become a public school teacher. The Minister of Education, although he survived the vote by a slim margin, nevertheless shared our perspective and resigned shortly thereafter.

We informed the Board of Trustees of our temporary need for housing and were informed of a stiff monthly rental with the stipulation that there would be no allowance for any period less than a full month. This generated immediate action and we moved to an apartment hotel in less than twenty-four hours. This experience confirmed our good judgment in preparing for the new mobile life style!

For two years I served as Urban Chaplain of The United Church of Christ in Chicago. The Chicago Association, The Community Renewal Society and The Board of Homeland Ministries created the position. The assignment was to nurture new forms of ministry and new forms of the Church. It was exactly what I wanted, but it never really came together. Secular groups were too involved in urban issues to theologize about "God's work in the city" and church members, even groups of the disenchanted within the institution, were disinclined to launch forth on urban mission.

Besides this, the approach was too fragmented. I believe mission is enhanced by the total experience of the fellowship. To attempt urban mission without the guidance and support of a Christian community, seemed to me, ill advised. Consequently, with pressure from no one, I resigned.

Deciding what to do next presented a problem. I had no credentials, no academic, professional or technical skills. In fact, a ministerial background seemed to be more of a handicap than a help. No one was interested in employing a ministerial reject and at 52 years of age I was not disposed to initiate an extended program of reeducation or retraining in a professional field.

The urgency of the situation led to an examination of a variety of franchises (from McDonald's to Stuckeys to Cobbs), sales jobs, career counseling, real estate management, gift shoppes — the whole gamut including dozens of possibilities. Fortunately, the University of Chicago offered me a position as Campaign Associate in a $160 million capital campaign.

(Despite my unreadiness for retraining this initiated a training program which has at times been rigorous and has never stopped.) A year on the campaign led to becoming Associate Director for the solicitation of corporations and foundations and the year following I became Director of Development for the Division of Biological Sciences of The University of Chicago. This included development responsibility for the Division of Biological Sciences, The University Hospitals and Clinics, The School of Medicine, Director of the Program of Continuing Medical Education and Director of The University of Chicago Cancer Research Foundation. It involved wearing a rack full of hats and running a department of about 15 employees and a lot of volunteers.

For the past two and one-half years life at Franklin and Marshall College in Lancaster, Pennsylvania as Director of Planned Giving has been considerably less demanding and quite satisfying. Franklin and Marshall claims that it is in the first ranks of the nation's independent liberal arts institutions and there is a measure of satisfaction in being associated with a quality institution. Lancaster is a beautiful community located in the eastern population corridor of the country, close to New York City, Philadelphia, Baltimore and Washington.

During these eight and one-half years annual compensation has compared favorably with the ministry. Salary has increased year by year, except once involving the last move. Fringe benefits are comprehensive and generous. Evenings and weekends are free. Pressures, especially as compared to the Christian fellowship are minimal. There is satisfaction in being part of the educational community.

Being cut-off from the ministerial role was disconcerting, but not insurmountable. Mostly I've missed the fun and excitement of growing intellectually, emotionally — totally in the company of a Christian fellowship. Institutional boredom, limited income, the hurt and pain of conflict are worth the price of sharing in an authentic fellowship if it's available. But it's a rare thing and if one has enjoyed this experience even briefly he should consider himself fortunate.

My wife and I are not active in any church. In Chicago we were associated with The Church of the New Covenant, composed largely of those who withdrew from The First Congregational Church of Elmhurst and who for more than eight years have been a "buildingless and professionally leaderless" fellowship. The fact that 8 or 10 clergy in the First Church moved or withdrew, most of whom have been associated with this group accounts for much of the style of The New Covenant. Members do now, seem to be wholly satisfied with what they are doing, but appear to be held together partly by the lack of acceptable alternatives.

In October 1973 The Chicago Association of The United Church of Christ revoked my ministerial standing.

The invitation to this meeting caused me to re-read "The Local Church in Crisis." It consists of records and memoranda strung together with brief editorial comment. It is accurate. A member of "the opposition" is quoted on page 28 as saying: 1. The study was well written, 2. The documents were valid and 3. The sequence of events is accurate. I concur.

But to give this account "homiletical structure" I want to make three points.

1. It should be recognized first that this account reflects the situation from within. The documents were not originally composed to interpret the story to non-participants. There was much left out, much implied that nevertheless needs to be understood for a real evaluation of the situation.

"The Statement of the Minister" for example on pages 19 and 20 was written to support a statement from the Chairman of the Diaconate and the moderator in response to "the oppositions" demand that the ministry and the Official Board of the Church abandon the current program and revert to assorted activities and "good fellowship."

"The Minister's statement beginning on page 19 says, "There are many ways in which the Church can function. Anyone of a hundred New Testament images of the Church provides clues and directions. I am eager to change and grow with the congregation using any one or all of these images as a guide. Ideas and suggestions will be most welcome."

I was prepared for all sorts of flexibility provided, of course, it included a serious effort to be the Church. That objective was not negotiable. But that was the issue.

I had been using a New Testament image very extensively in attempting to work out a model for Churchmanship. The image was "The Body of Christ," the tangible, enfleshment of Christ's living spirit alive and working in a company of people motivated by a sense of having been "called" and "commissioned" through their affirmation of the Christian faith. As "the body of Christ" the Church has certain essential functions or life style.

I was willing to abandon that particular image, but to suggest adopting **any** of the New Testament images of the Church was just as unacceptable to the opposition. The question was were we intending to be a Church or an assortment of social groups.

It was the start of the journey and not the specified route or the final position that concerned me. I was of the opinion then, and am now, that you don't arrive at a destination, or achieve an intended result by proceeding in a way that is inconsistent with the desired end. One must proceed slowly, make necessary accommodations and digressions, but the goal and destination requires a willingness to take a first step in the right direction. Then there are all sorts of alternatives in determining the next step.

In "The Local Church in Crisis" there is a section called "A Style of Ministry" in which a former layman described my ministry by saying "You knew that he was struggling with something and that he saw in a sense a great truth. All he was asking us to do really was to get into this thing with him and start considering some of the things that are basic rather than the superficial piety and moralistic stance that Christians have held generally through the years . . . Here was a man who was not just talking at us or laying the thing out in front of us saying, 'This is what you ought to be doing.' Certainly, he was saying this, but he was himself constantly involved to the extent that you were always aware that he himself was really struggling with these things.

I don't believe study groups have understood this from the written account and yet it was clearly the issue with the participants in the Elmhurst situation.

2. A second observation is that the account in "The Local Church in Crisis" lacks local color. Arthur Herzog writing his version entitled "Onward Christian Elmhurst" in his book "The Church Trap" supplies some of the local context and thereby adds to an understanding of the situation.

He writes: "Some say that Elmhurst surreptitiously advertises the absence of Negroes and that its freedom from racial conflict is one reason real estate values are so high. Most Negroes can't afford to live in a place where the **average** income is $10,000 a year. Elmhurst, as the Chamber of Commerce announces, a little too loudly, is the "Largest City in DuPage County (Wealthiest County in Illinois and Fourth Wealthiest in the Nation)." The town, like the county, voted for Barry Goldwater in 1964. It thinks of itself as arch-Republican, stable, community-minded and religious.

"Elmhurst has a Church Street, and there, or on streets immediately by, almost every Protestant denomination is represented. Steeples vie with steeples, bells with bells, pastors with pastors. Of these churches one of the least imposing happens to be the most prestigious, **the** church of Elmhurst, the old brick and stone building of the First Congregational United Church of Christ which counts among its parishioners the town's leading politicians, a good part of the country club set and some of the richest and oldest families." Such was the basic flavor of the situation.

A personal anecdote may illuminate the picture. Sometime within the first month of my arrival in Elmhurst I called on the Chairman of the Stewardship and Missionary Education Committee with whom I had no previous conversation. When I called she appeared agitated and before I was seated she began:

"You should understand that this congregation is not going to be stampeded into a high pressure financial program. These people are intelligent and good and they won't take kindly to Madison Avenue promotional methods. Furthermore, this business of mission can be carried too far. There is plenty to do right there without worrying about Chicago, or some foreign country."

Someone had provided this woman with a lurid and frightening picture of my style of ministry and she was losing no time in getting on the offensive.

I responded by stating that "The Church is Mission." That is one of the "givens" we work with. However, a Stewardship and Missionary Education Committee has all the flexibility in the world in fulfilling its ministry to help the congregation channel its resources and energies in the most effective and creative ways."

But, the people of this church and this community were not about to consider the idea that "the Church is mission." One almost needed to be part of the local scene to make this assessment.

3. I have been told that "The Local Church in Crisis" has been used by study groups and judging from my own personal experience the general conclusion has been that competent leadership ought to have been able to "keep the lid on."

"If leadership had been more alert and recognized the situation earlier the crisis might have been averted."

If outside help had been engaged — help and counsel from the Christian community . . . . . .

If leadership hadn't proceeded so fast . . . . . .

If leadership had been more knowledgable of the realities of group dynamics . . . . . .

A study published by The Chicago Theological Seminary entitled "Conflict I" dated May 1969 states:

"The attempt to revise, within 2 or 3 years, an entrenched system which had built-up precedents over 75 years, strikes one as exceptionally naive."

Somehow I never came to that conclusion reading the prophets of the Old Testament or the events of the New Testament.

The question for me never was how to avoid the controversy and survive. Page 21 of "The Local Church in Crisis" quotes excerpts from a letter from me to a State Conference Minister who was considering me for a new church.

"The problem here (Elmhurst) is not a political problem. I am sure I can hold on by reducing it all to the least common denominator of interest and willingness to face the implications of the Christian faith. The heart of this church is quite united in a willingness to go along provided the major emphasis is achieving an overall concensus based on the lowest common denominator of understanding, interest and commitment."

So the primary question, for me at least, was not how to avoid being fired. That's fairly simple. The question was, and continues to be, how shall the Church survive? Not how shall a minister hold on to his job, but how shall the Church hold on to its mission?

I began my comments by observing: "Except for moral lapses and unethical behavior ministers are almost never fired." Maybe they should be!

From the accounts I have seen and from what has been related to me, study groups have not grappled with this problem. I believe this comes closer to the question of why so many — clergy and laity alike have chosen to pursue their way outside the institution.

70

A Profile of First Church
1966 - 1973

By Ernest H. Huntzinger

I received my copy of the June 1966 issue of **The Register,** the day prior to receiving a letter from the Pulpit Committee of First Church. I had read with interest the articles relating to "A Local Church In Crisis" the day before, but I turned then to consider them with critical study.

Four years prior, I had assumed the position of minister to The First Christian U.C.C. of Philadelphia, Pa., unaware that that congregation dismissed my predecessor. And, realizing the decided disadvantage of entering a situation with a minimum amount of insight and knowledge, I concluded that I would enter negotiations with First Church, Elmhurst, to gather information and to explore the possibility of entering a relationship with them.

During the period from that first letter, to the call I received from the Church, I read and studied First Church with close scrutiny, and was in turn, studied and scrutinized by the Church. So that, when I assumed the position of minister to the congregation of First Church, and took up residence in Elmhurst on February 1st 1967, we knew each other pretty well. But for the most part, what we knew of each other was a paper history, and while that has validity, it is no substitute for face to face encounters and relationships. So, in conjunction with the Diaconate of First Church, a dozen or so neighborhood coffees were held in homes to help my wife, Nancy, and me to become acquainted on a face to face basis with the membership. Those experiences resulted in very positive affirmations for a future together. While I felt encouraged and welcomed by the congregation, I had a less than affirming expression from my colleagues, one of whom stated that he was glad to meet me, but that he could not say that he was glad I was here. That was Dr. Merl Schiffman, then pastor of Bethel U.C.C., Elmhurst, who later became and remains a dear friend. From the mouth of one who shall remain anonymous, I overheard an inquiry made to one of First Church's lay persons, at an Association Meeting, "Where'd you dig him up from?".

I mention this not for the purpose of saying in essence "poor Huntzinger", I mention it because it is the clergy who passes judgment on situations in the wider fellowship, for what I think are rather obvious political reasons - the primary one being, the perpetuation of the clergy. When, in fact, we might more wisely address ourselves to perpetuating the life of the Church, which as the Body of Christ gives credence to the clergy, and not vice versa.

Therefore, when I address myself to the questions raised by Fred Hoskins (p. 27 **Register,** June '66) concerning specifically the situation back then at First Church, Elmhurst, I get a feeling that there's a duality of citizenship in Christianity. One citizenship reserved for the laity and another for the clergy.

That duality, if it exists in actuality or in feeling, can strike a staggering blow to Christianity. If there is a lack of evidence that the church I serve is aware of sin, then I, too, come under that indictment, for I am a part of the church by the laying on of hands, not apart from it by the act.

And, if the identity I project as a clergyman is by and large in accord with the image the congregation has of me, then we share - then it is we work together, dance together, cry together. That has happened in my relationship with the people in First Church.

I turn now from this very subjective scenario to assess the aspect of renewal as it applies to First Church. This analysis like most sermons and all Gaul, is divided into three parts: Part I will consider a historical perspective. And, in this study we will attempt to examine its self-image. Part II will focus upon the standards by which the church lives. Here we will attempt to measure comparisons between the church as it actually exists, to the defined standards. In other words, how does the church measure up to being a church? Finally, Part III will explore the process of renewal - i.e., the way in which the church renews its life.

A HISTORICAL PERSPECTIVE

According to the record of written accounts, 1966 was a distressing year in the life of the church. The membership declined by two hundred twenty-one (221) persons - moving from a total of 1,430 members in 1965 to 1,209 by years end, 1966. Church attendance was down from an average attendance at Sunday worship services from 313 in 1965 to 271 in 1966. The congregation contributed a total of $102,200 in 1965 and provided a missions disbursement of $18,400. That is, a total of 18% of the budget was given to missions. In 1966, the congregation contributed $83,600 - approximately $20,000 under what was given in 1965. From that, 11% was designated as mission giving, for a total of almost $9,400.

The impact was obvious - an attrition of 220 members; the loss of $20,000 in revenue; the cut-back in missions to one-half of what was given the previous year; 42 people less in the congregation each Sunday - the church was in a period of great stress.

It might have been that the primary thought of the church during this time concerned survival. What was identified by the interim pastor, however, was that there was "an atmosphere of uncertainty and apprehension."

The interim pastor was Dr. Frederick W. Schroeder, President Emeritus of Eden Theological Seminary - a responsible theologian and an able administrator who related to the church as one committed to its life.

From his report to the congregation reflecting on the year 1966, one can determine the leadership he provided. His was not simply a support ministry, he supplied information for the church to gain in-

72

sights into its nature and purpose. He did not allow for self-pity, but he did afford a ministry of caring, as a servant of Christ.

He identified the church as an institution, and with that identity he included the following: "All of us know that the institutional church has been under fire in recent years. It has been accused of being so institutionally-minded as to be irrelevant. To some of us it seemed at times that there were leaders within the church that were prepared to liquidate the institution in order to get on with what they considered to be the Christian mission. Evidences are at hand that the tide may be turning. Though rather grudgingly, some critics of the institutional church have admitted that the Christian mission can hardly be discharged without some kind of an institutional entity, if nothing else, the mission of the church is dependent on the financial resources provided by local congregations. It is important, therefore, to maintain strong, stable congregational units for both worship and work. The Christian mission will surely fail if the spiritual vitality in the local church is below par. There is no need, therefore, to be apologetic in seeking to advance a congregation's growth in membership, to keep its facilities for worship and work in good repair, to operate with a balanced budget, and to foster a Christian fellowship that will draw all members closer together in the bonds of mutual understanding and a common purpose. The various boards and organizations of First Church have endeavored to do this . . ."

Such nurturing, such sharing in real time, afforded a substantial foundation for building the ministry I was able to bring to First Church. As was indicated earlier, my ministry was begun February 1st, 1967. During that year the most obvious concern centered about a pronounced absence of people in the 45 to 55 age bracket. Those whose children are sufficiently grown to take care of many of their own needs; those whose job positions are relatively stable; those whose residence in the community is secure; those people who can devote the time, provide the talent, and who can share the responsibility of the work the Church is called upon to do.

This is not to say we had no one representing that crucial population in the church. It is to identify a very few who were part of that category - those who were, occupied the positions of leadership and upon them fell the lion's share of work and responsibility.

They performed well. Their commitment was to the church and there was little evidence of one person imposing his will upon the church. There was a sharing and an emerging self-awareness on the church's behalf that projected a positive future.

The years since that time are not uneventful, but for the sake of moving on, we will identify in passing some of the land-marks that stand more pronounced in the fields of the past.

The membership for the years 1967-70, contained an unusual proportion of people close to retirement. The church, therefore, because of that factor and along with a culling of the roles that took place during 1970, reached its low in membership statistics - that low is registered as 962. As of December 31st, 1973, the membership of the church now stands at 1,051.

It was also during the year 1970 that the church achieved its highest mission giving ratio since 1965, having contributed $16,400 out of $97,800 - for almost 17% of its total receipts.

In the fall of 1971 the church completed a major renovation and building program. As a result, the record shows a decrease in mission giving to 14% of total budget in 1971, a decrease to 9.8% in 1972, and an increase in 1973 to 10.1%, when we received $116,600 in contributions and disbursed to missions $11,800.

In concluding this historical perspective, the church moved from breathing an atmosphere of uncertainty and apprehension to a position of self-worth. If there had been a "country club" posture assumed by the church as was charged against the church in times past, that posture is no longer evident. It is a vital institution, and its present health projects a joyful future.

We move now to Part II which is prefaced by the title -

CHRISTIAN STANDARDS AND CHURCH LIFE

The church as it is known now, endeavors to measure its life against the standard of God's love for the world through Christ. It's to become aware with Chardin, that "the way we treat people is the way we treat God." It's to embrace Paul's commitment to the Church as the Body of Christ. It's to keep trust with each other to provide the means for Christ-like expressions in our world.

So, as we reflect, as we look ahead, our greatest concern must show evidence of our love for and understanding of people. This we reckon as a divine commission.

This is not to suggest that we cannot disagree. There are people within the church whose outreach is as long as their arms are long. For the most part, however, there is a desire for the church to bear witness to Christ-like expressions.

Most of the membership bears witness through their contributions, but a substantial portion also serve by way of board and committee responsibilities in the church. Others, through offering their time and talents provide tutoring; a number of others participate in delivering hot meals to those incapacitated in the community. A sewing group within the church has committed itself to the unglamorous but necessary role of providing called for items for Church World Service, and for other community projects.

A few years ago two of us from the church served on the Neighborhood Services Board in Chicago, and I was an active participant in placing before the Elmhurst City Council support for an open housing ordinance.

The point of all this is to state explicitly that First Church accommodates diversity. There is no judgment leveled against those who choose to restrict their Christian witness and no pressure is brought to bear upon those who choose to proclaim theirs.

During the building program there were those who felt that the money might be more profitably spent in the inner-city. Others opted for even more money to be spent on the structure. There were open forums provided where opposing views could be aired - and all were encouraged to speak what was felt.

As anyone who has been involved in an extensive building program knows, there are more than casual brushes with some rather chaotic situations. Yet, there was not one person who left the church because of that program. The differences were resolved with reason and regard for one another.

During the years since 1968, study groups were formed treating as subject matter, contemporary theology; black history; Christain witness; drug abuse among our young people; and so on. Projects such as the Christian Action Ministry Project sponsored by the Social Action Committee, brought into focus areas of help we can provide in the inner-city. And, during the past year, we affiliated ourselves with the Pastoral Counseling Ministry of Oak Brook, to make available counseling services for those in our membership in need of long-term help, but who do not possess the financial means to receive it.

This year, we have established a Living Endowment Fund within the church. These funds will be available to individuals or groups in the church who seek to participate in personal growth seminars, family life retreats, and educational and leadership training opportunities which apply to working within the Church. In this way we hope to develop a wider base of committed lay leadership.

Therefore, as we seek to measure the life of the church against the standard of God's love for the world through Christ; as we keep trust with each other and show evidence of being a caring community, we show evidence also of belonging as legitimate heirs to the Body of Christ.

We turn now to Part III which is abbreviated by way of Paul's admonishment - "Brethren, the time is short." Part III will consider the subject matter of -

CHURCH RENEWAL

In looking back upon the events and issues of the past eight years, one must readily conclude that a report of the activities of the church cannot be separated from the events and issues of the world. We were affected by the Viet Nam War; we were anxious witness to Kent State; we were stunned and saddened by the violent death of Martin Luther King, Jr. We continue to be distressed about the abuse of young bodies on dope and older bodies on smoke and alcohol. We have become alarmed about the desecration of the earth, and how it is we have taken advantage of its air and polluted its waters. We know of the SLA, Watergate, and find less and less to verify the democratic process by way of the present administration.

In all this, wholesale opportunities for new values are urged upon us and our children. From television and radio, from newspapers and magazines, we feel the strain of the old in conflict with the new, the enticing sway of the secular drawing us from what is sacred. And the question is posed, "Who shall determine the course of our destiny?" Shall the media? Shall the administration? Shall the military? . . . Well, what about the Church?? . . . Can we find renewal there? . . .

Obviously, it does not have all the answers, but it does provide both an atmosphere and an opportunity for people to share, to build trust, to provide hope, and it might be that the renewal process it provides for its members might also provide renewal for our world. A renewal process that starts from the premise that only insofar as we participate in hopeful endeavors can we have hope; only as we share with others can we expect others to share with us; only as we establish trust in our world can we expect to receive trust.

We have learned during these years that the church can accommodate diversity without disintegration. We have experienced a growing process by the free exchange of ideas, and we have seen evidence of a forward movement though a faith rooted and grounded in God's love as that love is by us shared.

Beginning next fall, we will embark upon a new relationship between staff and congregation.

During the past seven years we have had two ordained people who shared the work of the church. Next fall, we will have one full time clergyman; a director of Christian Education, whose primary responsibility will be the Church School; a director of Youth Activities, one whose job description will focus upon Junior and Senior High programming; a parish visitor; and, a teacher for adult classes in religion-oriented study.

Hopefully, this venture, along with some structural changes in both the Diaconate and Board of Christian Education, will result in some form of renewal.

This then is a brief sketch of a church set in the midst of the world and striving to serve. It is **a place** to which people can repair and find a renewed strength; it is **a way** by which lives can derive purpose; it is **a people** who seek with what means we have to build a better world.

STATISTICS — FIRST CONGREGATIONAL U.C.C.
Elmhurst, Illinois

			Membership	
1965 Receipts	$102,201.26		1,430	
1965 Missions	18,408.86	18%	313*	21.8%
1966 Receipts	$ 83,580.27		1,369	
1966 Missions	9,370.44	11.2%	271	19.7%
1967 Receipts	$ 92,916.57		1,209	
1967 Missions	11,231.09	12%	338	27.9%
1968 Receipts	$ 94,188.12		1,144	
1968 Missions	15,060.66	15.9%	308	26.9%
1969 Receipts	$ 97,164.01		1,135	
1969 Missions	16,156.97	16.6%	335	29.5%
1970 Receipts	$ 97,799.63		962	
1970 Missions	16,418.10	16.7%	256	26.6%
1971 Receipts	$ 93,651.01		1,026	
1971 Missions	13,167.42	14%	321	31.2%
1972 Receipts	$ 95,794.94		1,050	
1972 Missions	9,413.65	9.8%	333	31.7%
1973 Receipts	$116,594.28		1,035	
1973 Missions	11,778.00	10.1%	303	29.2%

Pledge Units in 1973 - 329   *Average Sunday Attendance

The
Covenant
Church of the New Covenant

Elmhurst, Illinois

We are a Christian church, founded in response to God's initiative in love, and initiative witnessed to in the Scriptures as they relate to the history of Israel and proclaim the fulfillment of that history in the man Jesus of Nazareth who through his life, death, and resurrection is revealed to us by the Holy Spirit as the Incarnation of God, His love, and His person.

We confess and proclaim that Christ has set us free from the bondage of sin and death unto a life of freedom, a life that reaches into eternity. We recognize that·if we are of Christ we are a new and redeemed humanity. The Scripture puts this in the most radical of terms: "You are a chosen race, a royal priesthood, a holy nation, God's own people, that you may declare the wonderful deeds of him who called you out of darkness into his marvelous light" (I Peter 2:9). Such words press hard upon us, for when we look to ourselves we do not feel ourselves worthy of such titles. Yet we know that, worthy or not, these are the names by which we have been named and we must seek to open ourselves to the enabling power of God's Spirit so that even we might be made into such people. Therefore, hoping to be open to His coming and to His grace, WE PLEDGE OURSELVES in freedom as individuals and as a congregation to the following discipline:

1. PRAYER
The Scripture enjoins us to pray constantly, and Jesus assures us that "God will vindicate his elect who cry to him day and night" (Luke 18:7). In the light of these and other injunctions WE PLEDGE OURSELVES to private and family devotion and to regular attendance in the corporate worship of this congregation.

2. STEWARDSHIP
Jesus told one rich young man to sell all he had and give the proceeds to the poor. While we know that this is not a law for all to follow, it does indicate the quality of Christian stewardship. Therefore, WE PLEDGE OURSELVES to give of our substance and time to the church until it is actually true that our life's blood is in the Church.

3. MISSION AND SERVICE
We recognize that life in the church -- the fellowship and the joy and

the mutual upbuilding thereof -- is not for its own sake alone, but for Christ's commission to the Church for the proclamation of the Gospel to all mankind. It is not enough to proclaim Christ's Word; we must also do it on behalf of others. WE PLEDGE, therefore, to give of our time as well as our substance toward the proclamation of the Word and the amelioration of human need in all its terrible forms, sparing not ourselves.

4. CHRISTIAN EDUCATION

WE PLEDGE to open our minds to understand God's will and purpose in the world and to share with one another in study and dialogue. Jesus once rebuked his disciples, whose zeal would keep them from him: "Suffer the little children to come unto me." WE ALSO PLEDGE OURSELVES, those who are parents with children at home, to religious instruction in the home, and those others, to cooperate in all ways possible with this crucial task, as Christian Education is a function of the whole church.

5. MUTUAL UPBUILDING

WE PLEDGE OURSELVES to submit to the counsel and correction of other Christians offered in love. We cannot discipline ourselves without the help of others. The "priesthood of all believers" can never be achieved unless we submit ourselves to the priestly mediation of fellow Christians.

6. OUR RELATIONS TO OUR ENEMY

Christ requires of us that we love our enemies. In him we have come to know that the greatest love is God's love. Therefore, we shall strive through the help of His Grace to reflect His love to every other human being, to those who by reason of their race or socio-economic class, or personality or culture might present to us the face of an enemy. We shall seek the courage, as Christ told us, to turn the other cheek to enemies real or imagined ("turn him the other also" - Matthew 5:39); and we shall seek their good, not our own, for in Christ all good is already our possession.

7. CHURCH AND STATE

Although we are to "render to Caesar the things that are Caesar's," Christ would also have us render "to God the things that are God's" (Mark 12:17). We recognize that if we are in Christ, ours is not just a task of passive acceptance of all that "Caesar" does. Therefore, WE PLEDGE OURSELVES to seek to realize that the judgment of God might even be upon our own nation, and we seek to discern God's judgment in all situations in which our nation finds itself. "No man can serve two masters."

Elmhurst, Illinois
May 1, 1966

A Profile of the
Church of the New Covenant

By JOHN W. HANNI

Dr. Hoskins' criticisms orginially published in the **Chicago Theological Seminary Register** in June of 1966, pointedly called our attention to important deficiencies in First Congregational Church of Elmhurst, as well as, the group that eventually became the Church of The New Covenant. To some extent I see the formation of The Church of The New Covenant as a response to these deficiencies. It must be said that we of The Church of The New Covenant were probably not aware or articulate regarding our identity until after the fact of our organization. In a long series of meetings the group together wrote a covenant agreement, as well as a constitution for the congregation, and it was through these meetings and the formation of these two documents that we attempted to address ourselves to such issues as church discipline.

Our smallness in some ways has been an asset. We were originally 70 members and now are 30. Most of the decrease has been accounted for by retirement, job transfers and deaths; but only a small number have left because of disaffection with the congregation. Our size has permitted closer personal relationships within the congregation. Our size has dictated that almost all members assume some specific responsibility for the congregation. In this sense the sharp demarcation between church leadership and followers has been rather blurred. We now find ourselves at a point in our history when it is actually difficult to do all we feel we should be doing as there are too few of us to assume responsibilities. We are currently evaluating our congregational life by means of a committee on evangelism, one on Christian education, and one on worship and by consulting the minister of a sister church. It is quite possible that the congregation will, as a result of these studies, elect to go out of existence.

Another rather unique asset in our congregation has been the presence of at least four ordained clergymen who have secular jobs, so are not professional clergy in the sense that they are salaried and dependent on the church. All four of the current members of the clergy are on the staff of the Elmhurst College. As a result of this, we have more than our share of skilled theological guidance for the size of our congregation. The clergymen members of our group like this arrangement because if affords them full membership in the congregation. Another asset has been our policy to support mission activities in which our own members participate. This has not been entirely the case because one large item in our budget has been support of The United Church of Christ. Approximately half of our mission giving has supported mission activities in which members are directly involved, so there is direct feedback from our own members regarding these mission activities. In spite of these above enumerated assets we are forced to be realistic about ourselves. We are relatively weak, maybe dying, but most of us consider that the effort of the last eight years has been worth it. We are limited in what we can do in a number of respects, but we have been able to participate to some extent in the larger church. Perhaps one of the things that we have done best is to respond to the needs of each other within the congregation during life crisis situations such as death, illness, and family problems. One aspect of this mutual support is a clear awareness of individual assets and liabilities along with the necessity for acceptance and tolerance.

One example of this acceptance and tolerance is that sooner or later almost all members of the congregation participate in the planning and conduct of worship. Worship services therefore vary from very traditional to the quite unusual and the range of services is characterized by an equally wide-range of effectiveness. But in general when the quality of a worship is poor it is tolerated because it is generally accepted that that service represents someone's best effort. Our congregational life has gradually evolved in the direction of an emphasis on confession, prayer, dialogue about the scriptures (often taking the form of discussion following the Sunday sermon), active participation in mission (with at least two-thirds of our budget going to mission), Bible study, and finally an effort to integrate all of the children of the congregation into all activities of the church.

There are issues that cause disagreement in the congregation. Examples would be that some members feel very strongly about the denominational affiliation, whereas others would be perfectly willing to go their own way. There are some that feel that the lack of a hired professional staff does not actually provide effective ministry to members of the congregation in need of one sort or another. At times there is some controversy about some of the innovative worship services as opposed to the traditional. We seemed to live in rather constant disagreement because we are usually able to openly discuss such issues, in spite of the fact that these discussions often do not arrive at resolutions, but simply an awareness of our differences.

ADDENDUM

On the 25th of March 1975, the Executive Committee decided to call a special meeting of the congregation for the 20th of April 1975 for the purpose of discussing whether or not the congregation can continue to exist in its present form. Our membership is now down to 22 and could well be diminished further than that within the next several months because of the retirement of people within the congregation. We have gotten to a point where our manpower shortage to do the things that need doing is critical, and in the past couple of years our participation with the larger denomination has become nil except for our financial contributions. There has been some discussion of maintaining our identity as a study group, but with members formally joining other churches. At this point, I would say that it is rather probable that we will cease to exist as a congregation this year. (At the meeting on April 20 the congregation reaffirmed its covenant and decided to continue its existence with a new thrust on evangelism. Ed. note.)

"It Has Been Worth It"

By RONALD GOETZ

When Perry LeFevre asked me to participate in a forum about the aftermath of the split up of the First Congregational Church of Elmhurst, I took the occasion to reread an article I had written at the time for the now defunct **Renewal** magazine. This article described the history of the First Congregational struggle and the subsequent founding of our new church, the Church of the New Covenant. The article came as quite a jolt as I was somewhat dismayed by my earlier confidence that the over-whelming proportion of the right was on our side. Issues between Christians are rarely that clear.

I was also somewhat surprised by my earlier confidence that something of widespread importance for the greater church was taking place here in Elmhurst. Events have served to deflate any grandiose illusions I might have been harbouring. None of which is to say that I have any real regrets about the new church or my family's involvement in it. It has been an edifying and upbuilding experience on the whole. I have learned a great deal about the Christian faith through my participation in the congregation and I have witnessed some moments where the work of the Holy Spirit seemed very immediate and sure.

I recall, for example, during the founding stages of the congregation, the way in which we attempted to establish a basis for some genuine discipline and accountability. I had imagined that the way to go in this matter was toward a standard of doctrinal adherence based upon a biblical theology. I discovered, and was not surprised by the discovery, that many of our members were quite uninformed in questions of the Bible. Beyond this, some of their theology I found to be dreadful. However, I also believed then and now, that the Holy Spirit was truly at work among us and certainly within these "heretical" brethren. Surely we could not deny His presence or postpone our recognition of His presence until we could develop structure by which these benighted souls be properly instructed in the "true" biblical faith. We could not put the Holy Spirit on the back burner. Obviously the urge for a disciplined life together arose prior to "good doctrine." It was very helpful to me to see, not only as a church member, but also in my work as a theologian, how subsidiary doctrine is. Of course there is a need to testify to the works of God in "clear and definite words." But if the Spirit is with the Church, these words will emerge. I have been much taken by the way in which the congregation has grown in understanding, but it was not from my, or someone else's, establishing a credal formula and then forcing adherence. It was by living together in the love of Christ that we have come to a more mature intellectual grasp of the faith.

A second interesting incident occured when the Black Manifesto was issued. It demanded a head tax on Christian congregations to be paid to the black community as reparations for the culpability of the Church in the institution of slavery. I happened to be assigned to preach soon after the publication of the Manifesto, and I spoke on its demands, pointing out that in spite of the Marxist rhetoric and flamboyant character, we as Christians ought to pay up. The sermon discussion that followed found the congregation split almost to a person on the issue. The debate was heated. After the service, people on both sides of the issue began calling one another and arranged meetings during the week. After an intense series of quite spontaneous meetings and debates, the church took a vote and the vote was virtually unanimous to send the money. This was in Elmhurst--one of the most politically conservative cities in America.

I am not certain that we were right, though I am sure we acted in good faith. What I was impressed with was the open, essentially non-doctrinaire spirit in which the congregation tried to meet the challenge. We met and tried to discover God's will for us. We met realizing the issue might split the church, but people felt with great intensity that they were personally challenged by the Manifesto and they had to resolve the issue one way or another. Too often when the Church takes a stand on social and political issues, it adopts the tone of Moses on Sinai and proceeds with a self-righteous, though often naive, confidence which is particularly obnoxious. I felt this kind of confidence blessedly lacking in the decision on the Manifesto. There was a profound sense that we did not know how to respond, but we had to respond in some way. May God have mercy on us. The Church has, on social-political issues, had the grace to live somewhere between naivete and cynicism. The members have been involved in concrete issues and in places of human need in a spirit of Christian realism, never hoping too much--never without hope.

As I have indicated, I have learned and profited personally, and I hope I have grown in the faith. But I have also been aware of certain weaknesses, the greatest of which has been our failure to grow or even to hold our own in terms of membership. Our numbers are dwindling and there are a number of reasons for this--some quite beyond our control, as for example, the fact that there are a number of well established churches already in the area.

One of our weaknesses in this respect grows directly out of one of our strengths. Because we are a tight-knit group, because there has been considerable sharing and openness and even confession of sin--through the years new people in our midst have tended to feel that they have intruded upon a family gathering and have entered the picture so late that they could never be fully incorporated. I don't believe this exclusiveness is a genuine problem, but I understand how the concern could be felt.

It is a cliche among those concerned with evangelism that evangelism is the work of laymen and to a large extent, this is true. I am confident that the members of our church have let their light shine in the world and have made a difference in the lives of their neighbors. There is a difference, however, between affecting a person's life and involving that person in the fellowship of a particular church. This usually is the function of one (to put it bluntly) whose job depends on drumming up a continuing membership, i.e., a professional clergyman. Since no one's job depends on it, we of the New Covenant Church can say with imperiousness, "Even if the church were to fold tomorrow, it has been worth it." Such an attitude is comforting but hardly conducive of growth.

Another issue that concerns me is the high proportion of theologically-trained people in our church (at least five in a congregation of 30 or 40 people). We once styled ourselves a lay led church and while in one sense this is true, in another sense we are well served, perhaps even over served, by the clergy. I don't think we have reached that point, but unless we begin to seek more members, we are likely to become a society of ex-preachers preaching to one another.

Part IV Appendix
The Church In Conflict—Three Cases

Conflict in Middle City

By CHARLES A. DAILEY

(This case study is designed to illustrate community conflict and to provide experiential learning through two group role plays)

THE setting for this case is Middle City, a midwestern metropolis of more than one hundred thousand people in which earlier riots in the ghetto had generated widespread fear. These riots destroyed people, property, and trust but they had been the source of consolidation of the black community. A coalition of black organizations was founded called POWER (Power, Opportunity, Win, Equality, Respect). Its leader, Minister Flowers, initially produced some small gains for the members which were drawn from all the Negro organizations and associations in the city. Twelve hundred delegates attended its first convention in 1967.

The President, Minister Flowers, was an aggressive outspoken leader, bitterly critical of the white power structure. He had been greatly influenced by Malcolm X. He was an early advocate of Black Power. The city itself is heavily industrial. Jackson Industries is the largest employer. It has wide influence in the community, and it was one of those companies which early declared itself to be an "equal opportunity employer." About 3 per cent of its employees in 1968 were Negro; the population of Middle City is about 10 per cent Negro. However the 3 per cent represents a sharp gain over the Negro proportion at the time of the riots.

Whatever Jackson Industries' previous record in race relations or in industrial relations (it is not unionized), its top management did meet frequently with the leadership of POWER, beginning in 1967, regarding what might be done about the city's disadvantaged population. Other community interests were concerned with these same problems and with the emergence of POWER. The Council of Churches had generally supported POWER feeling that as the united effort of the black organizations it could deeply influence the well-being of the city.

THE EMERGENCE OF THE CRISIS

In September, 1967, the POWER President asked the President of Jackson Industries if the company would hire five hundred people who would not meet hiring standards and train them. Jackson Industries agreed to talks. These ran on for four months. The Jackson President who had participated personally earlier, then designated an assistant to continue the talks. This was in December.

With the Hammer Corporation, POWER had earlier come to some agreement. From Hammer, Flowers had demanded two hundred jobs, but had settled for fifty. He had asked for no agreement in writing. There appear to have been trust and some amiability. Later Dixon Vance, a Flowers' associate, said of Hammer Corporation: "We wound up laughing at the same jokes. With Jackson Industries we were never on the same wavelength."

While POWER was not happy about the Assistant Vice President's designation as negotiator for Jackson Industries, they nevertheless proceeded to negotiate. On December 20, he signed an agreement with POWER which appeared to provide for the hiring of five hundred hard-core unemployed. POWER released an announcement to that effect to the press without clearing with the company. Two and a half days later the Jackson President, Harrison Dillard, publicly voided the agreement.

Among the Jackson objections to the announced agreement was the exclusive recruiting channel through POWER. (POWER denied that this was part of the agreement.) President Harrison Dillard called a press conference and declared that the company had been under an unjust and savage attack. He believed that the question of jobs was simply a screen for a drive for power in the community by an agitators' organization.

THE JANUARY NEGOTIATIONS

During January, there were further meetings between POWER and the executive committee of Jackson Industries. There was a breakdown. POWER claimed that the committee stood them up for one of the meetings, and that it attempted to pawn off underlings to negotiate who lacked authority. Jackson's statement was that it met with POWER, but when Jackson attempted to have

POWER negotiate directly with the officials responsible for employment and training, then POWER refused, describing these officials as "janitors."

The Council of Churches

The Council of Churches took out a full page advertisement in the morning and evening papers. It reprinted the agreement which the assistant vice-president of Jackson Industries had signed with Minister Flowers in December. Though there was division within the Council, this was an attempt to get Jackson to reconsider. More overtly expressed division followed. There were several resignations. The hostility developed by these actions was felt when efforts were made to raise the budget in the spring. Pledges to the Council were down almost 20 per cent. At the same time some support came from outside the community at least in the form of verbal approval by some distinguished church leaders.

The Denominations

The denominational groups were inwardly divided but a majority within each of them favored continued support for POWER, holding that the company had been irresponsible in breaking its agreement, that justice demanded new opportunities for the black unemployed, and that POWER was the most representative and responsible organization in the black community. The company thereupon became less amenable. It declined mediation, attacked POWER's rejection of its own negotiators in calling them "janitors." Minister Flowers of POWER sent an angry telegram to Jackson Industries which implied violent consequences when summer came.

The Feelings in Middle City

Public opinion in Middle City was reflected in a survey taken several weeks later. It showed that most of the city's whites favored racial integration in both housing and in the schools. However, the opinion was that POWER had made the relations between white and Negro more difficult, that it had not improved the situation of the Negroes, and that Jackson Industries was right in its dispute with POWER (almost twenty-four to one). No similar survey data are available for the black population of Middle City. Two regional executives of a national black service organization did, however, challenge publicly POWER's right to represent the black community.

By February the situation in Middle City was becoming more widely known. A *national* denominational agency was led to denounce Jackson Industries for voiding its hiring agreement. It not only commended POWER, but pledged its total effort to bring Jackson Industries back to the bargaining table with POWER.

But within the same denomination there was disagreement. A local executive, John Williams, took the approach that behind-the-scenes discussion, coupled with public evidence of a successful community action program involving many organizations and resources beyond Jackson Industries alone, would shift the focus of the dispute to a problem for Middle City and not just for Jackson and POWER. Williams would not say that he or his associates (an informal group of church and other community leaders) were attempting a mediating role. But they had been working together.

At the same time Robert Harkness, an executive of a national agency of the same denomination objected to the committee's make-up. He said it lacked people who understood the problems of the very poor. Harkness implied the committee was merely an attempt of the power structure to "save face" for the city and for Jackson Industries. It did not reflect equally great concern for the poor. Other national groups became concerned for what was happening in Middle City, and the national media began to take notice. National black power leaders visited the city and denounced the "racist" policies of Jackson Industries.

CIVIC DIPLOMACY

Early Probing

In January, a group of church leaders, including John Williams, a denominational executive; the Episcopal Bishop; and Henry Slocum, President of City College, began meeting informally to see what could be done. They intended to involve persons from industry, hopefully including Jackson Industries, and from the black community. Their approach was to organize a community effort to deal with the problems of jobs for the disadvantaged and to avoid any direct attempt to mediate between the two parties.

They were able to determine informally that Jackson would not be uncooperative. POWER took the position, however, that they were interested only in direct negotiations with industry, particularly with Jackson Industries. They appeared to question the motives of this informal group—perhaps they were merely trying to get Jackson off the hook?

The informal group faced an early decision. What good could be done by further effort if POWER were not a part of it? They moved to continue to inquire into the possibility of a community-wide organization which would solve the job problem, but they made it quite clear to POWER that they could not and would not attempt to move without POWER.

A series of meetings began at the College. These were kept out of the press. The reasoning was that premature publicity had exploded the original Jackson-POWER negotiations and that the situation continued to be delicate.

STOP: *Assign January roles to individuals and role play a committee meeting at this point* (pp. 7–11).

The March Series

John Williams wrote letters to a number of persons inviting them to serve on a Citizens Committee which would develop a community-wide approach to inner city problems—especially unemployment. He listed nine members of an interfaith group which had been meeting informally for seven weeks. No mention was made in these letters to either Jackson Industries or POWER.

On March 8, a fifty member group assembled. It included the interfaith group, the local head of the State Employment Service, and representatives of POWER, the Council of Churches, and various companies including Jackson Industries. This group in turn constituted an eighteen member planning subgroup which included representatives from POWER. The tone of the meeting was positive. There appeared to be a willingness to cooperate. The press was absent at this exploratory meeting.

The planning subgroup was to organize a proposal for jobs for blacks by March 20. It met several times. It set April 11 as the deadline for organizing a corporation to mobilize all available community resources against unemployment. But Flowers protested the manner of organization. He held that the poor themselves did not really have a voice in the planning. And he denounced the failure of any commitment of a certainty of jobs yet forthcoming from industry. John Williams gave a mild mannered reply to the effect that the group's work was still at a preliminary stage and that criticism was premature.

PLANNING FOR THE APRIL 11 MEETING

What could be done to bring POWER into the organization which would be formed April 11? A response to the criticism that the poor were not sufficiently represented was developed. The Proposed Board of Directors of the new organization (to be called Jobs, Inc.) was originally to include twenty persons, as shown in the accompanying tabulation. A revised plan, shown in the right-hand section of the tabulation, was prepared.

JOBS, INC., BOARD OF DIRECTORS

Original Plan		Revised Plan	
Industry.	10	Industry.	10
Representatives of the Poor. . .	5	Representatives of the Poor. . .	7
Clergy.	5	Clergy.	3

The further question was how to ease the tension between POWER and Jackson Industries, since that might be an obstruction to the formation of Jobs, Inc. Somehow the leaders of Jackson Industries took initiative. The President of Jackson sent a letter both to the committee and to Minister

Flowers indicating that his company was willing to work with POWER within the new framework to develop programs to reach the hard-core unemployed.

STOP: *Simulate a committee meeting using April roles* (pp. 11–15).

Jobs, Inc., was formed April 11 with its Board of Directors constituted according to the revised plan. It was agreed that the new corporation would train, recruit hard-core unemployed through various community agencies. Industry quotas would be worked out later. POWER however was not fully satisfied. It declared its intention to force the original issue at the annual stockholders' meeting of Jackson Industries.

THE ANNUAL STOCKHOLDERS' MEETING

POWER bought ten shares of Jackson Industries stock so that it could attend the annual stockholders' meeting on April 25. Flowers and twenty-five other POWER members sat in the audience. Representatives of a number of national bodies of several major Protestant denominations withheld their proxies. They attended prepared to ask questions.

When the meeting began, Minister Flowers was on his feet immediately. "We'll give you until two o'clock to honor that agreement." He left the meeting. At two, his group returned. Flowers asked, "Are you going to honor the agreement? Yes or no?" The Chairman said, "No." Flowers walked out of the meeting with his group. Outside, he told his group: "In ten days we'll have a mass picketing of Jackson Industries. If it's war they want, war they'll get."

Back at the annual meeting, the Chairman presented Jackson's position. He reviewed the company's past record in equal opportunity, its dealings with POWER, and its continuing intention to provide training and employment for disadvantaged people. A few days later POWER seemed to adopt a more moderate position. The Council of Churches reacted uneasily to the new situation. It adopted a resolution in which it disapproved of public demonstrations, pointing to the dangers associated with the coming anniversary of the earlier riots at Middle City.

MAY AND JUNE

What would be the agenda of the May meeting of Jobs, Inc.? There appeared to be two major issues. Could each industry accept a quota of new workers? Should the poor who were to be hired be given jobs first and then trained? The position taken by POWER was that training offers were not enough. Real job guarantees were imperative.

Jobs, Inc., met. It elected the twenty member Board of Directors, but not without objections voiced by Flowers. Jackson Industries felt that the movement was toward a workable compromise. A commitment was being made by all Middle City industries together, so that they could adjust the quotas for hiring among themselves from time to time.

As the June meeting approached, the informal group which had created Jobs, Inc., found through its behind the scenes contacts that direct discussions between POWER and an industry group, including Jackson Industries were feasible. Direct talks, serious talks, began between the heads of several companies, including Jackson, and Flowers. They met three hours on June 19; they had phone conferences on Tuesday; they met four hours on Wednesday, five hours Thursday night. The negotiations ended that night after nine or ten calls to clarify exact wording of the agreement.

An agreement had been reached—Jackson would send interviewers into the black community in cooperation with POWER. There would be periodic meetings between Jackson and POWER to keep things moving. POWER would motivate the hard-core workers. There was no mention of a particular number of jobs to be guaranteed. But Flowers felt he had an agreement. When his POWER convention assembled, he was able to read a telegram from the President of Jackson Industries. The telegram acknowledged that POWER spoke on behalf of the aspirations of the black poor. Hearing that affirmation, the convention broke into cheering. They chanted "We won" and marched around carrying signs.

In retrospect, some observers said that the turning point was reached when several company presidents who had stopped meeting with POWER began to do so again. Others said that POWER decided to trust the men who formed Jobs, Inc. Still others thought that the change came in the attitudes of the leaders of Jackson Industries. Still others said that Flowers decided Jobs, Inc., would succeed and that POWER had better get aboard. Whatever the cause of the turn in events, the ground for cooperation had been laid.

JANUARY ROLE PLAYS

John Williams
Denominational Executive

Your Situation in January

You are aware of the community importance of the negotiations between POWER and Jackson Industries, and of the role of the Council of Churches in supporting POWER. You have up to now supported the role of the Council of Churches, but have not otherwise involved yourself in the problem. Your role as a community leader, among other church heads, has been up to the present to stand by for help to anyone who will use it, to resolve a crisis of common concern.

For this reason, you were hesitant to leave town for Christmas, but family demands call you to Minnesota. You leave on December 21, after learning that there has been an agreement between POWER and Jackson Industries. But when you arrive in Minneapolis, you learn that the highway police between Middle City and Minneapolis were trying to find you to urgently request you to call your office. When you do call, you learn that Jackson Industries has disapproved its agreement and that the city's leaders are all apprehensive. You are urgently requested by various key persons in the Denomination to take a stand of some kind.

What will you do? Consider the pros and cons of each of the following courses of action:

—stay out altogether, hoping that the two sides will see you as a potential mediator
—stay out altogether (the church can only harm its own cause by becoming involved in these complex issues)
—line up with the Council of Churches by making a public statement "calling a spade a spade" and raising public pressure on Jackson Industries to change its position
—some other course of action?

Having chosen a course of action, proceed to set it in motion among some or all of the following persons: the Council of Churches' Executive; the Jackson Industries' President or a representative; the head of POWER. If your course of action is to stay out, you may either inform these persons of your position, or may say nothing and wait for someone else to make the first move.

Among your advisers are two associates from the Denomination's office.

Roger Bevan
Associate of the Denominational Executive

Situation in January

What has led up to this situation has been the crisis precipitated by Jackson Industries' repudiation of its agreement with POWER on December 20. You believe that the Denominational Executive, whom you advise, must take an immediate and positive stand. The situation is dangerous, for either violence or irretrievable deterioration in relations between Whites and Blacks. You are afraid the Executive will remain on the sidelines, as during the last few months. This is the time for a stand.

Counsel him on the course of action you believe you should pursue. This action can involve him in direct statements to, or discussions with, any of the

94

following other persons: the Executive of the Council of Churches, the Jackson Industries, or the POWER head.

Once he has made his decision, assist him in carrying it out.

Raymond Evans
Council of Churches Executive

Situation in January

You are in a severe bind. Your board is split over the wisdom of going further to support POWER. The majority want to do it, but there is a powerful minority, including some Jackson Industries employees who feel you have done enough.

Your position is that if POWER cannot win this dispute with Jackson Industries, then it will lose its leadership over the Negro community. You will be back where you were, with a disorganized and an even more dangerous ghetto. You must go down the line with POWER. And if the denominations weaken your position by making it appear that there is no moral case for POWER, you will be in an even more untenable spot.

You might bide your time, or come up with some more active proposal to help POWER, or talk to John Williams to get him to stay out of the situation and not make your problem more difficult.

James van Dusen
Council of Churches President

Situation in January

You are President of the local Council of Churches, a lay leader widely respected. It has been your policy to support Raymond Evans, the Executive closely. You respect his idealism and hard work.

It does not seem to you to be the business of the Council of Churches to intervene in any dispute between a business corporation and another organization, such as POWER. You believe it is going too far to take sides in the dispute between Jackson Industries and POWER. You believe Jackson Industries tried seriously to negotiate with POWER, and you know that POWER has launched many attacks on community organizations which appear to be intemperate and unwarranted.

Ultimately, the only real pressure you can bring to bear on Raymond Evans is to resign. Perhaps that won't be necessary. However, tension is rising in the community and you haven't decided what you will do. The majority of the Council of Churches board is going to support Raymond Evans, just about whatever he does.

Minister Flowers

Your Situation in January

Your leadership is in a shaky position. First of all, it was extremely difficult to build POWER, and it was hard to show any tangible results for all the effort. What had really been done for the Negroes of Middle City by POWER? Then, just when you felt that a great battle had been won—when Jackson Industries had signed the agreement on December 20—Jackson Industries pulled the rug out from under you by repudiating you. This proves what you have suspected a long time about the "White power structure." It also justifies Saul Alinsky's argument that you have to go in and *take* what you intend to get.

You are therefore going to keep the pressure up on Jackson Industries. You are also not going to talk to underlings next time—only the word of the top man is enough for you. You also want to be able to say to your followers that your organization, POWER, is big enough to force the big corporations to talk directly and seriously with you.

You are going to insist on the original terms. There has to be a set number of jobs for the poor of Middle City, and those people have to be recruited by POWER. This is the only way you can keep "Uncle Toms" like the Urban League out of the picture, and it is the only way you can keep the Settlement Houses from ruining everything you have been building up. This is the time to get tough and to take a very hard line.

Dixon Vance
Flowers' Associate

Your Situation in January

You and Minister Flowers has fought hard to develop POWER, as the only really tough organization representing Negroes. Right now, it looks like POWER has bitten off more than it can chew. If Jackson Industries won't talk to you, what can you really do about it?

Your complaint is not so much that they won't give you the concessions (the specific number of jobs you demand, and the right to recruit for those jobs) you demand, but it is more they way they act. It is hard to talk to Jackson Industries' people. You think they are snobs. The other big companies in town will be tough with you, even shout back and forth, but at the end you can make jokes with them.

Harrison Dillard
Jackson Industries' President

Your Situation in January

Your Chairman of the Board tried, without success, to negotiate with POWER all during the fall last year. Finally, he decided to turn it over to an assistant V.P. Unfortunately this assistant V.P. grossly exceeded his authority in making the agreement on December 20. He conceded on the several points which Jackson Industries refused to concede before he took over. You instantly repudiated the assistant V.P.'s agreement. Anyone should know that only the head of a corporation can make such an agreement.

After the unfortunate publicity following your repudiation, you again tried to negotiate. When it became clear that the negotiations were to go on for many sessions, and were getting into details with which only your industrial relations department was familiar, you designated your industrial relations manager to represent you in talking to POWER.

They insulted him and refused to talk seriously. You cannot, as Company President, permit yourself to be compelled by this group—who have repeatedly engaged in this insulting behavior with other community organizations— to be at their beck and call for an endless series of sessions. Nor will you permit them to abuse or take advantage of your men. Jackson Industries has done a great deal for this community. You will continue to do a great deal—especially for the disadvantaged people. But it is not essential that it be done through POWER.

APRIL ROLE PLAYS

Raymond Evans
Council of Churches Executive

Situation in Early April

The pressure has worsened. POWER now proposes to make some kind of demonstration or confrontation at the stockholders' meeting of Jackson Industries on April 25. They want to know what national church support you can line up for them.

You have received strong hints from other local Protestant leaders, not necessarily conservative ones, that the demonstration at the annual meeting won't help the progress of their delicate mediation between Jackson Industries and POWER. They feel they might be achieving some progress, although you can't see it. They plan an organizational meeting for a new group named "JOBS" on April 11. You will go but will continue to support POWER.

The dissension within the member denominations and churches of the Council has greatly increased. Your budget is in serious trouble. The conservatives are in full cry after your scalp. You can't see that POWER has achieved any progress in its dispute with Jackson Industries, but can you weaken your support for them at this critical juncture?

Edward Croft
State Employment Service

Situation in Early April

You are the State Employment Service head in the Middle City area. Among your most important problems has been lining up jobs for the disadvantaged, and finding ways in the community to get them trained. You were making slow but steady progress in this, when the Jackson Industries-POWER dispute erupted last December.

You have not been involved on either side. However, local industry heads trust you, and you have been talking quite a bit with the Protestant leaders who have been developing a community organization which they propose to call Jobs, Inc. The organization would be headed by a board which has ten industry representatives, five representatives of Negro organizations, and five clergy. This appears sound.

The question is how to deal with the most crucial meeting of the group—on April 11, representatives of industry, the Negro organizations, and several Protestant denominations will meet and attempt to organize formally. Among the issues are whether the board will be accepted (especially by POWER) and how to get Jackson Industries onto the board. Jackson Industries simply won't commit itself to any specific long-range program for the disadvantaged.

John Williams
Denominational Executive

Situation at the Beginning of April

Everyone has been telling you that POWER and Jackson Industries cannot be gotten into a serious negotiating position. However, your experience with the resolution of apparently impossible labor-management disputes tells you that nothing is really impossible. But how to do it?

You want now to prepare for the meeting April 11, at which you and your group will attempt to form JOBS. The original plan calls for JOBS to recruit disadvantaged people for local jobs, to line up support among industry for this plan, to see that the people are trained. You want to get industry to commit itself to a set number of jobs (at least 1,800) within a definite time span. But you want to be sure that Jackson Industries, as the major employer and industrial leader, is included.

You also want POWER to commit itself to work for its aims within JOBS, rather than outside it, making demands.

At this point, your colleagues, including especially the President of the college and the Episcopal Bishop, have agreed with you that the following organization structure could be proposed:

JOBS would be headed by a community-wide board on which industry would have ten seats: the representative of the poor, five seats (to be allocated among POWER, the community service agencies, and the Urban League), and the clergy five seats. The Jewish, Catholic and Protestant faiths will all be represented among the clergy.

Among the issues you see as potentially disrupting the April 11 meeting are these:

1. How shall the poor be represented?
2. How can Jackson Industries be brought into the board?
3. How to prevent POWER from walking out?

With the Bishop and College President, prepare a plan for the meeting and engage in any preliminary negotiation you think useful with the others.

Henry Slocum
College President

Situation in Early April

You have been working quite closely with John Williams, behind the scenes, attempting to find a basis for getting Jackson Industries and POWER back together. The best chance seems to be to develop a community-wide organization which they can then both feel able to join.

Some big donors to your college have been pressuring you to stay out of the dispute. Their view is that it has nothing to do with the work of the Church or the work of a college.

You will now meet with John Williams and the Episcopal Bishop to discuss the prospects of formalizing an organization to be known as JOBS on April 11. In preparing for the meeting you wonder whether there is advance work which could be done to bring in the Jackson Industries' President on a constructive basis. You have had frequent talks with him this year, and appear to have his confidence.

The Episcopal Bishop

Situation in Early April

You have been working quite closely with John Williams, behind the scenes, in attempting to find a basis for getting Jackson Industries and POWER back together. Whether they get together or not, it is apparent that some concerted community effort on behalf of getting jobs for the disadvantaged is going to be necessary.

You have not made up your mind about POWER yet, and have made no public statement about the justice of its claims, because you have a committee which has been investigating POWER. Early findings about POWER do not inspire you with much confidence.

Your role in the negotiating this year has been primarily to lend moral support to an uncommitted mediation team. You have been under fire within your Denomination from the younger group.

You will now meet with John Williams and Henry Slocum (President of a local college—not one of yours) to discuss the prospects of formalizing an effective community organization at a meeting on April 11.

Dixon Vance
Flowers' Associate

Your Situation in Early April

You have hit upon a way to get at Jackson Industries. Their annual stockholders' meeting is April 25. That is the time to hold a confrontation if there ever was one.

The Press and TV will be there. You can get sympathizers to march in from several college campuses. You can at least regain some prestige for POWER. You might even get Jackson Industries to give in, when they see what you are going to do.

At this time, there is a lot of talk about a new community organization known as JOBS. This organization is going to meet April 11, when they propose to form. You can't take anything seriously which ignores the basic issue—that Jackson Industries has never agreed to do anything specifically for and with POWER. Until they do, the poor people of this town have won no battles that count.

Roger Bevan
Associate of the Denominational Executive

Situation at the Beginning of April

It seems almost impossible that POWER and Jackson Industries can be gotten into the same community organization—"JOBS," as some propose to call it. Your problem is to help the Executive come up with a negotiating plan to bring this about.

You may contact any of the following persons, to help get positions adjusted, to prepare for the organizational meeting of JOBS on April 11: Jackson Industries; POWER; Council of Churches; other industry representatives; College President. You must agree on basic strategy with the denominational executive, and then assist in any way you can to set up this meeting so that it can have even a slight chance to be productive.

Minister Flowers

Your Situation in Early April

There seems to be some slight progress toward the formation of the JOBS organization. You trust the denominational executive who has been working on this. For one thing, he has made it very clear that JOBS cannot really be formed without POWER. You feel he understands your problem in getting prestige and recognition for POWER among Negroes.

However, JOBS is largely beside the point. You doubt very much that Jackson Industries is serious about participating. In fact, the whole thing could be used to lily-white-wash Jackson Industries by making it appear as if Jackson Industries were going to do something for the poor. If Jackson Industries were serious, why won't they agree to a set number of jobs?

There is another big problem with JOBS. It is going to be run by a board on which there are 10 industry representatives, 5 representatives of the poor, and 5 clergy. This looks very much like just another case of the White Establishment telling the poor Negro what to do, and solving his problems. You can't go for the Board as it is constituted. You still have got to show everyone that Jackson Industries can be forced to surrender by a tough, militant group.

101

Counsel the Rev. Mr. Parks

A Role-Play for Two People

A FELLOW Pastor, whom you do not know well, phones you in some agitation, and asks for an appointment. It appears he wants your counsel—especially yours, because you do not know him well, and can be more objective; especially now, because he does not want to get into a worse situation than he has just been through. We will call you "Counselor."

PARKS: In June (1968), my Council voted to relieve me of all duties (the next day) and gave me a 90 day notice. The Council's vote was supported by the congregation, 2 to 1. My problem is: I am about to go onto another church. Since what happened to me at Davis Memorial doesn't make sense, I can't honestly say I won't get into the same mess all over again.

COUNS.: Tell me about it. What started the mess?

PARKS: Well, it started before I got there. Davis Memorial had a poor relationship to the United Church of Christ. I knew that when I accepted the call. But after I told my former Congregation I was going to Davis, the Davis Council voted to cut the general benevolence to the United Church by about 90 percent. They were going to punish UCC for supporting FIGHT in Rochester. You know about FIGHT?

COUNS.: I'll say.

PARKS: When I arrived on the scene in the Fall (1967), I grabbed the nettle and faced the issue. I used all the persuasive force necessary to get the Council to rescind their benevolence cut.

COUNS.: Pretty fast action by you.

PARKS: Another thing I found out. The previous minister resigned in 1966 because the Board wouldn't let him invite a Negro minister into the pulpit.

COUNS.: Maybe it would be a good idea for you to stop here and tell me about the people of this Church. The area, and so on?

PARKS: They need blasting.

COUNS.: Let's start out by asking what they're like, in value-free terms, and then we'll get around to what they need.

PARKS: Well, it's a congregation of 850 on the south side. E & R background. Budget $68,000. Quite active people. They had put up a new building, but weren't using it for anybody except themselves, really.

They have odd expectations of a Minister. You are Herr Pastor. You carry out the ministry for everybody else. If you don't bother them too much, you are a fine Pastor. You are also an "employee."

COUNS.: What does the term "employee" mean to you?

PARKS: It means you can't do what you want. I mean, you can't do what you ought to be doing.

COUNS.: Can you give me an example?

PARKS: Soon after I got there, I moved some furniture. A committee had decided this should be done, so I did it. A Mrs. H (you'll hear more about the H family) wanted to know who had the authority to move things around.

COUNS.: Why did this upset her?

PARKS: I don't know, but I'll tell you why it upset *me*. My capacity to make a decision was being challenged. I wasn't about to say the committee had decided it. I said I moved furniture on my own authority.

COUNS.: Why was authority so important to Mrs. H?

PARKS: The H family is used to running things. Mr. H is an executive, longtime resident. He controls the purse strings—is the perpetual chairman of the Finance Committee. Does everything by threat and violence. Like the other two men in the little power clique, he is a lower-class ethnic type who happens to be making some money. Mr. H challenged me at the very beginning. I accepted that challenge. And he never did defeat me—I was too strong a man.

I know you're thinking I wasn't tactful. But you won't believe how things were. When I moved that piece of furniture, Mrs. H actually called me a thief. This may sound trivial and childish. Other people even complained if I wanted to change the letterhead—and when I wanted to break the confirmation class into two groups of ten, rather than keep it in one large group.

* * *

STOP: WHAT'S GOING ON IN THIS CASE?
WHAT QUESTIONS WOULD YOU ASK AS COUNSELOR?

The Counselor pauses here to make a few mental notes to himself. This pastor seems to react to challenge by placing himself in the very righteous role of Prophet. He is in a hurry, sounds that way as he talks. He does not react very sensitively to the great differences between this Congregation and the last one he had (last Congregation was full of professional people who expect an involved Minister with lots of flexible new programs).

The Counselor also knew the Rev. Parks' predecessor—a sensitive, soft-touch guy. A listener. Didn't push when he didn't have the political chips. Avoided issues—never talked race, for example, for a long time. He tried very hard to reflect the wishes of his people. I wonder if Parks knows what a contrast he is. And what that shock does to people—how long it takes to adapt to. If I resume this conversation, what can I really say that would be helpful?

* * *

COUNS.: Were there some people who supported you? How were you able to give them the kind of Ministry they wanted?

PARKS: There are always people who want to break up a clique which has been in there for a long time. These men had forced through a decision to build a $300,000 building. There was no real debate and it got through on a very narrow margin. A building they shouldn't have voted.

The trouble was, my support was slow to get going. A lot of people came out for me only after I had been voted out. One member came out at the meeting and said the ruling body was trying to scapegoat me. The problems they were blaming on me were there before I came.

COUNS.: How did they feel about your sermons?

PARKS: That is the most surprising part of all. What have you heard in this community about my preaching?

COUNS.: No question about it. You are well known as an extraordinarily fine expository preacher.

PARKS: Well, some said I was Johnny one-note on the race question, and others said I did nothing but preach the Bible.

COUNS.: How would you say the Congregation saw themselves as people?

PARKS: Helpless. They are blue collar people, used to being controlled. Feel left out of American society. No capital investment has gone into their community for 40 years, and yet taxes are going up, "to pay for the Negro." That's the way they feel. There are fifty hate groups there, in that community.

COUNS.: What effect did this have on the way they saw you?

PARKS: They actually thought I was going to bring a Negro into every block. I did not say such a thing. I did discuss open occupancy. I could feel the hostility at such times. And hear it.

COUNS.: Do you think you made any mistakes in this Ministry?

PARKS: I don't see how else anyone who wants to be a man could have handled it. . . . (*Pause*) I do remember when I first had a frank discussion with the pulpit committee, in which I refused to agree to continue using their present order of worship and refused to agree to continue to use only certain confirmation materials; I should have found out whether the Pulpit Committee had any real significance. The Council ignored all those agreements.

COUNS.: You spoke earlier of being regarded as an "employee." Does this mean the Council or others looked down on you in some way?

PARKS: On the contrary. In that tradition, they put the pastor on a pedestal. For example, I came out of the construction industry. I like to lift a hand. But when they saw me doing a little physical work, the members objected—said it destroyed my image as a minister, words to that effect. How do you account for that?

What do you say here? _____

_____

_____

Group Discussion Guide:

1. How do you evaluate the actions and attitudes of this minister?
2. What internal conflicts do you infer he is experiencing in this process?
3. Identify the strengths and weaknesses of this leader as a conflict manager.
4. What do you imagine was the effect of this conflict on the life of the congregation?
5. How do socioeconomic factors enter into institutional conflicts?
6. What alternative sets of attitudes and styles of action would you recommend to this leader for the future?

Pastoral Conflict with Extremism

(The story of one pastor's successful struggle with extremists
who tried to drive him from his church)

DID the extremists blow me out of the congregation? No, they did not. I stayed until victory was won and then I left. I had served for nine years in a suburban, midwestern congregation of 1,200, including a church school of 500. In the fall of 1967, the congregation did a self-study survey, with over half the members responding. Nobody objected to the music or the prayers (except the prayers of confession), but there were objections to the sermons and the Scripture on the basis that they dealt too much with the war and race issues. This was the first indication of unrest.

Reflection questions
* *What do you expect the pastor is feeling at this point?*
* *Is this what Charles Dailey calls an "early warning signal" of impending conflict? If so, what should be done?*

Things began to happen in October, 1968, when the young people observed Youth Sunday. They created a contemporary experience, involving service of worship with a rock band in the chancel, psychedelic posters, and flashing lights. They made testimonies about what the Christian faith meant to them. As a result of all this, some adults got up and left during the service. The minister was the youth pastor from our central state office. He came wearing a turtleneck sweater and a peace medallion. Boy, did we ever hear about that!

What would you do at this point?
* *Ensure that the youth do not repeat such a disturbing service?*
* *Make calls on the adults who left the service?*
* *Try to have the youth minister fired or at least censured?*
* *Do nothing?*

Three adults formally protested the youth service a month later. Then the president of the congregation asked me for an open-ended resignation. He said, "Something is going to happen at the next board meeting." He didn't know what, but something was going to happen, and he thought if he had my open-ended resignation, the whole thing could be solved then and there. I said I'd think about it.

How would you respond at this point if you were the pastor?

* *Write the open-ended letter of resignation?*
* *Write a letter informing the whole congregation of what is happening?*
* *Speak individually with board members prior to the next board meeting. If so, what would you say?*
* *Try to control the agenda of the next board meeting.*

The next board meeting was a sight to behold. There were 15 members of the church school board; 20–30 church school teachers; a large audience; two families who had come to make complaints about the church school curriculum; and a John Birch organizer and two members of a John Birch front organization from a nearby large city.

* *What has been happening in the congregation between the youth service and the board meeting?*
* *Is the meeting going to be confined to the original issue of the upsetting youth service? If not, why not?*

The complaint against the curriculum went like this: From the pupil's book, a woman read words like "can't be done," "impossible," "hardly ever," and "difficult," and then said, "See, that proves that the curriculum is all negative!" Then she picked up another book and went through "kill," "was murdered," "died," "life ended," and so on. "That proves the curriculum teaches violence and murder!"

After this attack on curriculum, as well as on confirmation resources and *motive* magazine, which is sent to our college kids, the complainants showed a 50-minute filmstrip, *Crisis in the Churches* (produced by a front organization of the Birch Society), which attacks the National Council of Churches, the World Council of Churches, the United Church, and Judson Church in Greenwich Village. By this time the church school teachers were burning up, wanting to say something. But they didn't get a chance. As soon as the attack was finished, one of the board members said, "Well, it's obvious we need to do something." He moved that we call a congregational meeting to vote on getting rid of the church school curriculum, throwing out the confirmation resources, reviewing the policies of the denomination at all levels, and taking a vote on whether or not I should be removed as pastor. There was no discussion of these issues; the vote to have the meeting was carried nine to four.

You are the minister. What will you do now?

* *Resign in protest—and hope that your strategic resignation will rally the congregation and reverse the tide?*
* *Organize a telephone and letter writing campaign among your supporters?*
* *Ask the Board to reconsider its action?*
* *Play it cool and do nothing?*

At next week's board meeting, the chairman of the board of deacons and the chairman of Christian education moved that the board reconsider the action of the previous weeks. That motion didn't get to the floor, even though it had a second and appeared valid. The president simply ruled it out of order.

The members of the congregation knew nothing about this until, 10 days later, the *Journal* published all the details, including names. The paper appeared at 2 P.M. By 5 P.M. the president of the congregation had every member of the church board in his front room except me. The president said he didn't know where I was. When I walked into the meeting uninvited, I was accused of putting the article in the newspaper; the church board was angry about having their names printed.

What had actually happened: Someone had written an anonymous letter to the newspaper, saying, "Our church has been attacked by the Birchers. Where can we get help?" There was no signature, but the letter was postmarked locally. The paper called me to find out what was happening. Then their specialist on Birch Society affairs began research, and the result was the article which exposed the whole situation.

From there on, people began making telephone calls to the men named in the article—the president of the congregation, the druggist who brought the film-strip, the dentist who made the motion—demanding to know what was happening. They asked questions like "Why are you accusing the pastor of being a Communist?" They called night and day. It became apparent to the congregation that something was awry and that elected leaders of the church were not representative of the people. At the next board meeting, the deacons demanded the rescinding of the motion calling for a congregational meeting. Again the president called it out of order.

This meant more massive calling around the clock. People canceled appointments with the dentist involved. The Catholic priest told his congregation, "I don't want any of you shopping over at that drugstore" (owned by the druggist involved). The Catholic church began having daily prayers for our church. They offered to provide pickets on the sidewalk!

Finally the board agreed to have twelve information meetings to investigate the curriculum, the confirmation resources, and the pastor.

At the next congregational meeting, the annual meeting, the nominating committee provided two or three extra candidates for every office that was open. The extremists came along with their slate—they dug up people who hadn't been to church for ten years and got them to run for the office of deacon or trustee or education board. The Birch people were sure they had it in the bag because they had rounded up 60 people for a meeting whose normal attendance was 90. But the church school teachers had done some work, too, and they had gotten 120 people there. When the voting took place, not one single Birch person was elected to office. They got their 60 votes, but they didn't get into office.

The whole story finally ended at a special meeting held to vote out the curriculum. None of the extremists showed up. Of the 80 people present, 5 voted against the curriculum, and everyone voted in favor of the confirmation resources and other resources of the church.

As a result of this attack, the congregation became much stronger. I'd been trying to get people to read denominational publications, but not until this attack did they. In my final sermon and comment with the boards, I referred to Joseph when he forgave his brothers. The brothers had meant it for evil, but the Lord had meant it for good.

Out of this attack and experience, that church is stronger today than it ever has been.

* *Under what conditions does conflict have constructive outcomes?*
* *Identify what you believe this congregation may have learned in this conflict process.*

Contributors

Ronald Goetz ia a member of the faculty at Elmhurst College.

Charles A. Dailey was on the staff of Dartmouth College when he wrote this essay. He is now Senior Associate, McBer and Co. and Research Associate, Harvard University.

Donald G. Stoner is on the staff of Elmhurst College.

William Dudley is on the staff of Franklin and Marshall College.

Ernest H. Huntzinger is minister of the First Congregational Church, Elmhurst.

John W. Hanni is a psychiatrist and lay member of the Church of the New Covenant, Elmhurst.

Perry D. LeFevre is on the faculty of the Chicago Theological Seminary.

2661 1